THEATRE ON TRIAL

THEATRE ON TRIAL

Samuel Beckett's later drama

Anna McMullan

New York and London

First published 1993
by Routledge
11 New Fetter Lane, London EC4P 4EE

Simultaneously published in the USA and Canada
by Routledge
29 West 35th Street, New York, NY 10001

Phototypeset in Linotron 10/12pt Baskerville by
Intype, London
Printed and bound in Great Britain by
TJ Press (Padstow) Ltd, Cornwall

British Library Cataloguing in Publication Data
McMullan, Anna
Theatre on Trial: Samuel Beckett's Later Drama
I. Title
822.912

Library of Congress Cataloging in Publication Data
McMullan, Anna,
Theatre on Trial: Samuel Beckett's Later Drama/Anna
McMullan.
p.   cm.
Includes bibliographical references and index.
1. Beckett, Samuel, 1906–   —Dramatic works.   I. Title.
PR6003.E282Z777   1992
842′.914—dc20   92–30605
                                              CIP

ISBN 0–415–05202–5

CONTENTS

ACKNOWLEDGEMENTS

I would like to thank Professor James Knowlson for his continual assistance and encouragement throughout the writing of this study. I am also very grateful for the unfailing help and patience of the Archivist of the University of Reading Library, Michael Bott, and his assistant, Francesca Hardcastle. My colleagues at the Sub-Department of Film and Drama, the University of Reading, have borne with me and provided assistance during the final stages of completion. I would like to thank Stephen Harper for the support and inspiration which shaped this project, my family and the long-suffering friends who have watched over its difficult birth, and especially my mother, for her unqualified support and encouragement.

The author and publisher would like to thank Faber & Faber Ltd and Grove Weidenfeld for permission to reprint material from *The Collected Shorter Plays of Samuel Beckett* (1984).

INTRODUCTION

Theatricality can be seen as composed of two different parts: one highlights performance and is made up of *the realities of the imaginary*; and the other highlights the theatrical and is made up of *specific symbolic structures*. The former originates within the subject and allows [his] desire to speak; the latter inscribes the subject in the law and in theatrical codes, which is to say, in the symbolic. Theatricality arises from the play between these two realities.[1]

Theatre is ever the presence of the absence and the absence of the presence. Both are component in its every motion, but until recently its motions have taken place within phonocentric limits. One might say that we have been witnessing in contemporary theatre, and particularly in performance, a representation of the failure of the theatrical enterprise of spontaneous speech with its logocentric claims to origination, authority, authenticity – in short, Presence. This motion amounts to a virtual deconstruction of the defining hierarchy that has sustained theatre since the Renaissance.[2]

Since the first critical essays on Beckett's writing appeared in the 1950s, Beckett has been hailed as a modernist, an existentialist, a dramatist of the Absurd and, more recently, a postmodernist, to mention only the most commonly applied labels. Beckett is one of many writers whose texts have been transformed into palimpsests by successive generations of critics, yet, as Roland Barthes claimed of Racine, he seems 'to have made all the new languages of the century converge upon himself'.[3] Indeed, Beckett's work foregrounds processes which are central to much recent critical theory: interrogating and challenging the dominant epistemological sys-

1

tems and values of Western patriarchal history, opening up the spaces erased or repressed by the dominant languages of that history. I shall be referring to a number of current theoretical discourses in my own dialogue with Beckett's texts, which is also a dialogue, or perhaps polylogue, with theatre and with theory. If critical theory poses contemporary questions to Beckett's texts, these in turn, rather than providing answers, continually question the meanings offered by theory. I believe it is because of the relentless questioning at the heart of Beckett's work that, even as we move towards a new century, new cultural climates and new theoretical discourses, his work still has the power to haunt us – making us reflect on our own critical performances, reminding us of the blind spots of knowledge and theory.

David Watson's recent critical study of Beckett's fiction suggests that the novels after *How It Is* 'inscribe a "theatrical" element of performance, initiated already in *The Unnamable*, onto the space of the narrative novel. But what is performed is the very act or process of enunciation.'[4] Indeed, Beckett tends to focus on performance as a mode of self-consciousness, in relation to his characters' attempts to stage their own presence (or absence) and in terms of the author's continual interrogation of the act of representation. *Waiting for Godot* broke many of the dominant dramatic conventions when it was staged in Paris in 1953, but in the drama after *Play*, Beckett experiments even more radically with the nature and limits of theatre. Watson states that the late fiction 'mimes its own mimesis and anti-mimesis'.[5] How much more true is this of the late theatre, which raises fundamental questions about the nature of theatrical representation and its relation to mimesis and anti-mimesis.

MIMICKING MIMESIS

Over the past century, the foundations of Western thought have been increasingly undermined as the authority and value of central epistemological concepts such as truth, presence or meaning have come to be radically questioned. In *Writing and Difference*, the French philosopher Jacques Derrida argues that the systems of meaning underlying Western epistemology are organized around a privileged, central space of presence (the residence of the *logos*) which assumes the authority to judge and determine truth, meaning and value:

2

> The entire history of the concept of structure . . . must be
> thought of as a series of substitutions of center for center . . . .
> Its matrix . . . is the determination of Being as *presence* in all
> senses of this word. It could be shown that all the names
> related to fundamentals, to principles, or to the center have
> always designated an invariable presence – *eidos, arche, telos,*
> *energeia, ousia* (essence, existence, substance, subject) *aletheia,*
> transcendentality, consciousness, God, man, and so forth.[6]

The concept of a central presence manifesting itself through the
word gave rise to a series of binary oppositions where the privileged
term is associated with the transcendental values of the *logos*, for
example: presence/absence, same/other, truth/falsehood, speech/
writing.[7]

The definition of art as mimesis can be seen as complicit with
the traditional Western logocentric order, since the essential quality of both the *logos* and mimesis is truth:

> Mimesis, all through the history of its interpretation, is
> always commanded by the process of truth. . . . The presence
> of the present is its norm, its order, its law. It is in the name
> of truth, its only reference – *reference* itself – that *mimesis*
> is judged, proscribed or prescribed according to a regular
> alternation.[8]

Theatre is often described as the art form where the laws of
mimesis are most firmly rooted, not only in relation to the processes of judgement and the revelation of truth before an audience,
but in relation to presence. Alessandro Serpieri describes dramatic
relationships – between characters or between characters and
objects or setting – as being established '*through deictic, ostensive,*
spatial relations. From this derives the involving, engrossing force
of the theatrical event . . . because the theatre is mimesis of the
lived, not the detachment of the narrated.'[9] Post-Renaissance Western theatre also 'strives to create the illusion that it is composed
of spontaneous speech, a form of writing that paradoxically seems
to assert the claim of speech to be a direct conduit to Being'.[10]
Yet if mimesis is ideally the disclosure of presence and truth
through appearance, it also offers the possibility of appearance
without truth – mere semblance or mimicry. For these reasons,
Plato distrusted mimesis and saw in theatre its most treacherous
form. Practitioners of mimesis, particularly theatrical practitioners,

may be at best guardians, indeed instructors of the truth, but for Plato they were inherently suspect, since they dealt in simulation and impersonation. Theatrical mimesis disturbs both the social and the ontological order:

> What Plato distrusts (what Aristotle only partially reinstates) is that mimesis implies difference – the copy is not the model; the character not the actor; the excited spectator not the rational male citizen, yet both occupy the same ontological space . . . . Understood this way, mimesis has little to do with the stable mirror reflection that realism inspires . . . the sign-referent model of mimesis can become excessive to itself, spilling into a mimicry that undermines the referent's authority.[11]

This theatrical undermining of the authority of mimesis is of particular interest in a theoretical climate in which the structure of logocentrism is being challenged. Instead of the hierarchical structure of binary oppositions ordered in relation to the central place of the *logos*, Derrida substitutes the concept of a decentred structure, where there are no fixed points of reference or certainty, producing a dynamic and unlimited play of meaning between terms:

> Henceforth it was necessary to begin thinking that there was no center, that the center could not be thought in the form of a present-being, that the center had no natural site, that it was not a fixed locus but a function, a sort of nonlocus in which an infinite number of sign-substitutions came into play.[12]

Theatrical mimesis as masquerade refutes the stage as a site of presence and truth, setting up a dynamic interplay between signifiers or 'sign-substitutions'. Indeed, Maria Minich Brewer sees theatre as a practical analogue of some of the fundamental operations involved in critical theory's deconstruction of the traditional laws of philosophy and representation: 'Theatre allows a philosophical discourse to shift from thought as seeing and originating in the subject alone, to the many decentered processes of framing and staging that representation requires but dissimulates.'[13]

Representation is doubly framed in Beckett's late plays, as the text constitutes the characters' attempts to represent themselves, to bear witness of their existence through their narratives. The *agency.*

fictional world of the plays therefore revolves around the production and performance of narratives. In many of the plays, these performances occur on a stage which is primarily a scene of judgement, but in others, the performances constitute rites of transformation or metamorphosis which resist the structures of identity and representation authorized by the dominant laws. The plays also draw attention to their own status as performances. In each case, the impulse or imperative to create order and coherence, on the part of the audience and the characters, is set against the failure of both the characters and the visual/verbal text to achieve the fixity and mastery with which the traditional structures of narrative and visual representation are associated.

Beckett's stages therefore expose the mechanisms and the masquerade of logocentric authority, but they also displace it. Many of Beckett's characters experience some obligation or imperative to 'tell the truth': 'something that would tell ... how it was ... how she – ... what? ... had been ... yes ... something that would tell how it had been ... how she had lived ... lived on and on ... guilty or not ... .'[14] This imperative may be externally imposed – Beckett's theatre often features tyrannical creators who attempt to exert control over the body or text of their creatures – but it also seems to be imbedded in the very structure and material of language and representation. However, Beckett's theatrical practice also mounts a continual assault upon the structures of representation which implicitly uphold the ontological or juridical authority of the logocentric order, using strategies of fragmentation and repetition, replacing the stable sign–referent relation with a multiplication of signifiers. A recurrent pattern in his plays is the establishment of binary oppositions (self and other, torturer and victim, truth and semblance, presence and absence) which are subsequently undermined through the performance. The plays work against the assumption of any definitive position of authority from which to determine truth, meaning or knowledge, for either characters or audience.

STAGES OF DESIRE

The theories of Jacques Lacan and Julia Kristeva are useful in linking the destabilization of positions of knowledge and meaning in Beckett's work to his destabilization of structures of identity. Lacanian psychoanalysis presents the subject's ability to signify or

5

create meaning as dependent on the assumption of a position of identity within the signifying Symbolic order of language and representation. The assumption of this identity by the child is in two stages. Firstly, the infant's identification with his/her reflection in the mirror initiates the Imaginary order, which provides an image of totality and integration in contrast to the infant's experience of the unstable mobility of the drives and his/her lack of motor control over the body. This *imago* of the integrated body becomes the model for the subject's ego, anticipating the subject's assumption of the signifying position of the 'I' within language:

> This jubilant assumption of his specular image by the child at the *infans* stage, still sunk in [his][15] motor incapacity and nursling dependence, would seem to exhibit in an exemplary situation the symbolic matrix in which the *I* is precipated in a primordial form, before it is objectified in the dialectic of identification with the other, and before language restores to it, in the universal, its function as subject.[16]

Entry into the Symbolic order of language apparently offers the subject an identity and provides access to the signifying systems and codes of the social order: 'The psychoanalytic experience has rediscovered in man the imperative of the Word as the law that has formed him in its image . . . it is by way of this gift [of speech] that all reality has come to man and it is by his continued act that he maintains it.'[17] The Symbolic is therefore associated with the authority of the paternal, logocentric law which guarantees identity, order and meaning: 'It is in the *name of the father* that we must recognize the support of the symbolic function which, from the dawn of history, has identified his person with the figure of the law.'[18] However, Lacan demonstrates that entry into the Symbolic order, while apparently allocating the subject a position of agency and control, actually condemns the subject to a perpetual exile and alienation, since the subject can only represent [him]self by accepting [his] disappearance and replacement by the signifier: 'I identify myself in language, but only by losing myself in it like an object.'[19]

The child's entry into the Symbolic, like the mirror stage, is dependent on separation from the mother. This awareness of separation initiates desire for the maternal body, a desire immediately censored by the *name of the father* (the *non/nom du père*), creating the unconscious, at the same time as it initiates the child into the

Symbolic order: 'the moment in which desire becomes human is also that in which the child is born into language.'[20] Lacan therefore stresses the fundamental incompleteness or *manque-à-être* of the subject, exiled from the original union with the mother and from the Symbolic order in which [his] desire appears as the desire of the other: 'It is precisely in [his] solitude that the desire of the little child has already become the desire of another, of an *alter ego* who dominates [him] and whose object of desire is henceforth [his] own affliction.'[21] As Derrida posits the destabilization of the sign-referent relation, creating a dynamic circulation of meaning along a chain of signifiers, Lacan destabilizes the subject–object relation so that desire is continually displaced along a series of substitutions for the original lost object. Whether these substitutions are enacted within the Symbolic (linguistic) or Imaginary (visual) orders, the subject is chained to a perpetual performance of his/her desire.

Kristeva takes up this notion of desire, but reformulates it as *jouissance*, the effect of the repressed semiotic drives of the maternal *chora*. Kristeva's Semiotic corresponds to the stage when the child is still intimately connected through the drives to the mother's body and constitutes a dynamic space which refuses and dissolves the fixed positions of the Symbolic:

> the drives, which are 'energy' charges as well as 'psychical' marks, articulate what we call a *chora*: a nonexpressive totality formed by the drives and their stases in a motility that is as full of movement as it is regulated. We borrow the term *chora* from Plato's *Timaeus* to denote an essentially mobile and extremely provisional articulation constituted by movements and their ephemeral stases. We differentiate this uncertain and indeterminate *articulation* from a *disposition* that already depends on representation, lends itself to phenomenological, spatial intuition, and gives rise to a geometry. . . . Our discourse – all discourse – moves with and against the *chora* in the sense that it simultaneously depends upon and refuses it. . . . Neither model nor copy, the *chora* precedes and underlies figuration and thus specularisation, and is analogous to vocal and kinetic rhythm.[22]

The Semiotic therefore continually underlies the Symbolic, drawing attention to signification as a process, rather than as a fixed system. However, the signifying order and the signifying self may seek to disguise that process and present themselves as already posited: 'a posited Ego is articulated in and by *representation* (which we shall call the sign) and *judgement* (which we shall call syntax) so that, on the basis of this position it can endow with meaning a space posited as previous to its advent.'[23] Psychoanalysis therefore outlines a continual drama within the subject between the order and imperatives of the patriarchal Symbolic and the disruptive dynamic of desire.

Theatre can also either present itself as an already constituted world or draw attention to the processes of its staging. The former practice can be seen as reproducing the model of a universe created and in all material respects abandoned by an absent creator who yet remains the guardian of the truth or meaning of the created world. Derrida points out the 'theological' implications of such a conception of theatre in his essay on Artaud, 'The Theatre of Cruelty and the Closure of Representation':

> The stage is theological for as long as its structure, following the entirety of tradition, comports the following elements: an author-creator who, absent and from afar, is armed with a text and keeps watch over, assembles, regulates the time or the meaning of the representation. . . . He lets representation represent him through representatives, directors or actors, enslaved interpretors who represent characters who, primarily through what they say, more or less directly represent the thought of the 'creator'.[24]

Theological theatre not only emphasizes the authority of the Creator, but casts the audience in the role of perceiver and judge, with the performance or performers on trial. It therefore requires various levels of competency or mastery on the part of creator, director, actor and audience. Keir Elam points out that the construction of a dramatic world depends on the spectator's ability to decipher the codes on which this presented world is based: 'the spectator is called upon not only to employ a specific dramatic competence (supplementing his theatrical competence and involving knowledge of the generic and structural principles of the drama) but also to work hard and continuously at piecing together into a coherent structure the partial and scattered bits of dramatic information that he receives from different sources.'[25] However, in order to create the illusion of presence and mastery, theological theatre seeks to deny its artifice, the processes through which it is both produced and perceived.

On the other hand, as in Plato's 'bad' mimesis, theatre can also foreground its own artifice. Indeed, Kristeva's distinction between the Symbolic and the Semiotic can be seen as paralleling the distinction sometimes made in performance theory between theatre as representation and theatre as performance: theatre which posits the dramatic universe as an already constituted world and theatre which disrupts the positing of that world and stable images of identity, emphasizing instead the construction and performance of scenes and roles: 'As long as performance rejects narrativity and representation, in this way, it also rejects the symbolic organisation dominating theatre, and exposes the conditions of theatricality as they are.'[26] On the one hand, Beckett exploits and mimics the theological structures of theatre, from the absent master in *Waiting for Godot* to the tyrannical figures in *Play*, *Catastrophe* and *What Where*, but on the other hand, his emphasis on the spaces, margins and processes of theatre exposes and undermines the authoritarian eye of representation.

Beckett's theatre can therefore be seen as the site of a confrontation between the attempt to assume a position of control and judgement in relation to the visual and verbal representations of self and the laws of representation in general, and the opening up of spaces which challenge and disrupt the construction of the roles posited by representation, including those of self and other, spectacle and spectator. Beckett's drama frames the operations of authority, but also stages the drama of a subjectivity which resists or exceeds the dominant codes of representation, questioning in the process the languages and limits of theatre itself.

PERFORMING SPACES

As deconstructionist and psychoanalytic theories underline, central to the challenging of the authority of the Symbolic is a different conception of space. No longer the unitary central space of the *logos*, but a series of shifting and dynamic spaces which continually interact with and challenge the established boundaries and limits of representation.[27] Such a conception of space is foregrounded in Beckett's theatre.

Beckett's plays do not open upon a world already ordered in a manner corresponding to the organization of space within a par-

9

ticular society or ideology. Rather, they open upon darkness – a semiotic space from which image and then speech will emerge. Beckett thereby emphasizes the process whereby the dramatic world comes into being and shifts the focus from the scene or activity represented to the processes and conditions of representation. On the one hand, this space acts as a frame: 'No matter what is stripped away of character, plot and setting, on the stage there always persists within the most reduced performance, a residual self-doubling – the stage representing itself as stage, as performance.'[28] On the other hand, the darkness which remains part of the performance, since the stage space in the later plays occupies only a small area of the stage, constitutes a continual reminder of that which escapes or eludes the framework of representation.

Space is also used to fragment elements of image and text, preventing the presentation of a totalized structure. In more conventional plays, the stage dialogue tends to refer to the actual situation of the stage present, and even recounted narrative tends to be rooted in the present of the stage. Beckett, however, deliberately differentiates the 'two levels of representation' which, according to Joseph Melançon, are characteristic of theatre: 'theatre ... can simultaneously call into play two levels of representation: the verbal and the scenic.'[29] Melançon cites Benveniste's distinction between the signifying systems of each level: 'The semiotic (sign) must be recognised, the semantic (discourse) must be understood.'[30] As Melançon demonstrates, this duality is an important source of tension in the theatre: 'the specificity of theatre, or theatricality, can be defined as the possibility of creating a positional semiotics syntactically dissociated from the discourse which semantically invests it.'[31] Such a dissociation is at the heart of Beckett's dramatic practice in the later plays, where the text, reduced largely to fragments of monologue, is deliberately played against the stage image. The focus shifts from the textual or diegetic fiction to the performance of text and movement on stage.

The elements of performance in Beckett's plays foreground the interrelated processes of production, perception and judgement: both through his characters' attempts to represent and perceive their existence as an image or a narrative, and through the structure and texture of the plays which foreground the production of visual and verbal signifying material for perception and judgement by an audience. In other words, Beckett's plays not only exploit but self-consciously focus on the internal dynamic of theatre and the power relations inherent within that dynamic.

Rather than recreating a coherent dramatic universe, Beckett's later plays focus almost entirely on the body. Even the apparently inanimate props that are used, such as the urns in *Play*, the lamp in *A Piece of Monologue* or the rocking chair in *Rockaby*, are in a close symbiotic relationship with the body. However, Beckett dissociates the body from its usual function of indicating an individual identity and focuses instead on the body as an image: produced, signifying, perceived. The bodies in his plays tend to be fragmented and denaturalized, mouths or heads suspended in darkness, the stark lighting and stylized costumes and gestures stressing Beckett's use of the body as visual material rather than as a centre of identity. Moreover, the frequent separation of body and voice decentres the subject by creating a position of perception and discourse outside of the body and establishing the body as an object of perception. The body therefore becomes the focus of a struggle for specular possession, as in the psychoanalytic drama of the mirror stage. The dynamic of this theatre of the body becomes a paradigm for Beckett's exploration of theatres of power:

> But the body is also directly involved in a political field; power relations have an immediate hold upon it; they invest it, mark it, train it, torture it, force it to carry out tasks, to perform ceremonies, to emit signs.[32]

However, Beckett not only presents the body as an object to be manipulated through the mechanisms of discipline and control, but also focuses on the body as site of desire – a space or dynamic which eludes or resists linguistic or specular control. Rather than an icon of identity, the body is presented as a threshold between self and other, internal and external:

> The 'body' is rather to be thought of as the point of intersection, as the interface between the biological and the social, that is to say, between the socio-political field of the microphysics of power and the subjective dimension.[33]

This concern with thresholds and border zones is reflected in the foregrounding of perceptual instability in the late drama. The use of an area of darkness to surround the stage image means that the image is never 'given', but must continually assert itself against the darkness. Indeed, as previously suggested, the stage darkness in Beckett's later plays is not a static, stable or unified space. As with structure and space, stillness and movement or speech and silence, the opposition between darkness and light is destabilized. Beckett therefore focuses on those areas which precede or undermine the establishment of fixed boundaries and categories. The role of theatrical lighting in the creation of these 'between zones' is of central importance, as Stanton B. Garner has demonstrated:

> Hovering between poles that it refuses to embrace, the diminished lighting in Beckett's late plays occasions perceptual instability, simultaneously approaching and resisting the extremes of full illumination, and the absence of light.[34]

The emphasis on perception foregrounds the processes of constructing and interpreting narrative and image by both character and audience, and underlines both the ontological insecurity of the characters and the provisional status of the forms on stage – between production and perception, between absence and presence and between text and performance. Indeed, while the theatrical stage is generally considered to be a privileged space of presence or of the 'present', rooted as it is in the 'here and now' of the stage, Beckett plays representation against presentation and indeed presence, working not only in and through the dramatic medium, but against it, challenging its boundaries and codes and undermining its supposedly characteristic properties. Rather than a place of presence, the stage becomes a space where the processes of representation are repeatedly staged.

Since the challenging of traditional structures of authority and representation is also a concern of feminism, my analysis has been informed by aspects of feminist theory. While feminist critics have been influenced by or have employed the theories of deconstruction and psychoanalysis, their work approaches these theories from a different perspective. An issue of central concern in a number of recent studies is the 'feminisation of the postmodern field of knowledge'.[35] Alice Jardine's book, *Gynesis*, deals specifically with the appropriation by male writers of those spaces generally omitted from or devalorized by Western codes of symbolization, spaces which tend to be marked as absences and rejected as 'other', 'the unnamable', 'death' or 'woman'. There is a danger that in rejecting authority, and privileging spaces of dispossession and loss historically associated with the feminine, the exclusion of women from power is reaffirmed and the existing structures of power remain in place. However, I would argue that, if Beckett has appropriated the feminine in his critique of the dominant laws of representation, his dismantling of the languages of authority may contribute to or be reappropriated by those who are working to displace the history of Western logocentrism. While Beckett's aesthetic does privilege failure and loss, many of the late plays are also exploring forms of authority not linked to mastery. Therefore, in his analysis and exposure of the ways in which authority operates through the signifying systems of language, representation and identity, Beckett's work makes a contribution to the search for alternative forms of representation through which a different conception of authority and identity might be articulated.

This study analyses Beckett's major late stage plays, from *Play* to *What Where*. I have used *Play* as a starting point as I believe it represents a significant development in Beckett's use of stage space. *Krapp's Last Tape* contrasted an area of light with a formless space of darkness, but the space of *Play* is both more abstract and more ambiguous. The lack of any specific representative function of the scenic space means that it assumes semiotic polyvalence: simultaneously representing a skull-space, purgatory, the void of death or simply theatrical space and formal ground. The use of a large area of darkness also heightens the interplay between light and darkness, already explored in *Krapp's Last Tape*. The continual shifting from light to dark in *Play* is characteristic of Beckett's construction of perceptual 'between spaces' in the later drama.

I have not dealt with the plays in chronological order. Beckett frequently returned to techniques, preoccupations, even phrases used in an earlier text and reworked them in a different context, so that there is little sense of chronological 'phases' within the later work. Rather, I have grouped plays according to the issues outlined in this introduction. The first chapter focuses on the parody of authoritarian structures of representation. The second is concerned with the erasure of presence in relation to individual identity and the materials of representation. The third looks at the 'feminization' of Beckett's dramatic practice, while the fourth examines three of Beckett's most poetic late plays. In these plays, authority is displaced in the interplay between self and other, and the performance of the text enacts a rite of passage between life and its other, death. Within each section, I have chosen to analyse the plays individually, as this enabled me to work through a detailed concrete analysis of each play, building up a series of concentric or overlapping analyses, rather than a linear or thematic treatment.

1

MIMICKING MIMESIS

Subverting patriarchal mimesis is what we might call mimesis-mimicry, in which the production of objects, shadows, and voices is excessive to the truth/illusion structure of mimesis, spilling into mimicry, multiple 'fake offspring'.[1]

There is still . . . nothing more dramatic than a trial . . . . There is a sense in which every performance is a trial, offering up evidence.[2]

Knowledge, in the Western philosophical tradition, has been associated with reason, clarity and illumination. It is concerned with the process of making the truth visible, the revelation of the subject of inquiry to the interrogating eye. In modern European history, the Enlightenment project aimed specifically to relate knowledge more closely to scientific modes of enquiry. Truth and knowledge were defined primarily in rational terms, reinforcing the rejection of that which cannot be comprehended and illuminated by reason:

The development of rational forms of social organisation and rational modes of thought promised liberation from the irrationalities of myth, religion, superstition, release from the arbitrary use of power as well as from the dark side of our own human natures. Only through such a project could the universal, the eternal and the immutable qualities of all humanity be revealed.[3]

Hence the propagation of forms of knowledge and representation which privilege unity, plenitude and the mastery or repression of that which cannot be known or *seen*. The very term Enlightenment

15

suggests the links between knowledge, vision and truth. However, some contemporary critics suggest that, while aiming at liberation and progress, 'the Enlightenment project was doomed to turn against itself and transform the quest for human emancipation into a system of universal oppression'.[4]

In *Discipline and Punish*, Michel Foucault demonstrates how the Enlightenment spirit of enquiry and mastery was applied to the surveillance and discipline of individual bodies by the socio-political structures of power and authority in Western societies: 'the exercise of discipline presupposes a mechanism that coerces by means of observation.'[5] The term theatre derives from the Greek word for 'to see', and indeed theatre has frequently dealt with the revelation of truth through the unmasking of false identities or assumptions before an assembled audience. Theatre as scene of truth can therefore be linked to the human drive towards the interrogation of self and species in the pursuit of knowledge and understanding. However, as contemporary revisions of the Enlightenment project suggest, the search for integrity and knowledge can become the will to dominate. The mechanisms of theatre may therefore reproduce the operation of power as judgement and spectacle.

Much of Beckett's theatre focuses on strategies of surveillance and spectacle – most of the bodies which appear in his plays are subject to discipline and cannot escape either the confines of the stage or the relentless glare of the spotlight. This is perhaps a major reason why the late plays are rarely performed in the round – precisely because of the way they set up a frame, offering that which appears within it as spectacle. Beckett plays on relations and levels of authority within the theatrical apparatus: the authority of the text, the author, the director or the audience. The body of the actor is frequently foregrounded as the material on which this authority is inscribed and displayed. Beckett's plays also draw attention to the act of spectating, and the power relations inherent within it. Theatre can therefore make a spectacle of the operations of power – exposing, mimicking and subverting its strategies.

The physical restriction of movement or of the physical body has figured in all of Beckett's plays. Vladimir and Estragon cannot leave the stage space – at least for the duration of the performance. Like most of Beckett's characters they are hampered by physical disabilities. In subsequent plays, physical disabilities or restrictions frequently eliminate mobility altogether. Winnie in *Happy Days* is buried up to her waist in the first act, to her neck in the second. *Play* seems to carry on where the last act of *Happy Days* ends. The three talking heads on stage have no power of movement. Each is held tightly in the mouth of an urn and rigidly separated from the others. Each head is also subjected to the operation of the Light, which rapidly switches from one head to the other. When each head is illuminated, it begins to utter. The heads do not have control over their own speech, which is 'extracted' by the Light.

More than in any of Beckett's previous plays, therefore, *Play* foregrounds the framework of discipline and control in relation both to the characters' bodies and to their speech. In *Happy Days*, the Light, accompanied by a bell, dictated the beginning and end of Winnie's day, but not the pattern and rhythm of her speeches. The enforced immobility of the heads and the use of the spotlight reinforce the connotations of interrogation, and even torture: 'M: Why not keep on glaring at me without ceasing? I might start to rave and – [*Hiccup*] – bring it up for you.'[6] This association of the drive to knowledge with the operation of power specifically upon individual bodies is explored in Beckett's last play for the stage, *What Where*, while *Catastrophe* focuses on the presentation of a silenced body as visual spectacle by a figure of institutional power. In these plays, therefore, the body is foregrounded as a locus of the struggle for control and mastery, either within the subject who has internalized the laws of identity and authority, or between the subject and the external modes of law and discipline. In particular, these three plays explore the structures of power operating within the mechanisms of narrative and spectacle – traditionally the raw materials of theatrical representation.

PLAY: THEATRE ON TRIAL

Play self-consciously refers to those operations of sight and judgement essential to the establishment of truth according to logocentric rules. The three heads are forced to relate their texts under the interrogation of the Light. The Light is therefore associated both with revelation and with judgement. Indeed, the play juxtaposes two levels of perception and judgement: firstly, the figures' narration of their life-(hi)stories in an attempt to 'be seen' and judged by the Light, and secondly, the play itself as a representation of those processes of representation and perception, to be perceived by the audience. While the first level stresses the attempt to present or perceive the lives of the characters as a coherent narrative, the second level continually undermines any attempt to achieve either visual or narrative coherence, and in the process exposes and parodies the mechanisms through which representation has attempted to master the fragmentary and the unknown.

In particular, Beckett's presentation of the body in *Play* and in subsequent plays belies any stable or unitary concept of self which the narratives may attempt to establish. Lacanian theory is once again useful in investigating the importance of the visual image of the body as guarantee of the unified identity and authority of the self. Lacan has identified the emergence of the concept of self with the 'mirror stage' when the child (mis)recognizes [his] 'self' in the mirror reflection of the body, perceived as a totalized whole, in contrast to the 'fragmented body' which [he] has experienced until then. According to Lacan, the desire for a unified self is inseparable from, and indeed is constituted by, the perception of the body as a unified, totalized image. Jane Gallop refers to the mirror stage as 'a turning point. After it, the subject's relation to [him]self is always mediated through a totalizing image that has come from outside. For example, the mirror image becomes a totalizing ideal that organizes and orients the self.... It is the founding moment of the imaginary mode, the belief in a projected image.'[7] It can be seen as a model and paradigm of the attempt on the part of the subject to achieve mastery of both the internal and the external worlds through representation, with representation itself predicated on the image of the 'whole' body. Lacan emphasizes that this impression of mastery is associated with the visual fixity of the image in contrast to the unfigurable mobility of the drives:

> The fact is that the total form of the body by which the subject anticipates in a mirage the maturation of [his] power is given to [him] only as *Gestalt*, that is to say, in an exteriority in which this form is certainly more constituent than constituted, but in which it appears to [him] above all in a contrasting size (un relief de stature) that fixes it and in a symmetry that inverts it, in contrast with the turbulent movements that the subject feels is animating [him].[8]

Lacan stressed, however, that this stable, unified image, which apparently unites the inner and the outer, l'*Innenwelt* and l'*Umwelt*, is an illusion, and by identifying with it the subject paradoxically condemns [him]self to a perpetual cycle of self-division and alien-ation:

> Thus, this *Gestalt* . . . symbolizes the mental permanence of the I, at the same time as it prefigures its alienating desti-nation; it is still pregnant with the correspondences that unite the I with the statue in which [man] projects [him]self, with the phantoms that dominate [him], or with the automaton in which, in an ambiguous relation, the world of [his] own making tends to find completion.[9]

Moreover, as Jane Gallop indicates, this totalized self-image brings with it a terrifying awareness of the fragmentation which it is supposed to replace: 'The mirror stage would *seem to come after* "the body in bits and pieces" and organize them into a unified image. But actually, *that* violently unorganized *image only comes after* the mirror stage so as to *represent what came before.*'[10] Indeed, Lacan has suggested that such an awareness of 'violent unorganization' continues to haunt consciousness and to threaten the self-mastery desired by the ego: 'this illusion of unity, in which a human being is always looking forward to self-mastery, entails a constant danger of sliding back again into the chaos from which he started; it hangs over the abyss of a dizzy Ascent in which one can perhaps see the very essence of Anxiety.'[11] The consciousness of a funda-mental disunity or 'abyss' appears within the Imaginary as images of fragmentation, and in particular, fragmented images of the body. This conflict between the desire for mastery, associated with whole-ness and coherence, and the actuality of fragmentation and incom-pleteness seems to be reflected in the text and structure of *Play*. While the text indicates the desire for or insistence upon a unified image/narrative of self, the play presents fragmentation and differ-ence on all levels, both within and between image and text.

The visual image of *Play* seems to reflect both the rigidity and the alienating effect of the *imago* – the body is literally turned into an object, encased in the petrified form of the urn, recalling Lacan's 'statue in which man projects himself' – and also the fragmentation of the splintered Imaginary. The protruding heads are severed from the rest of the body and the image itself is in three separate parts – Beckett specifies in the stage directions that the three urns should not touch. Even more radically than in the preceding plays, *Play* resists investing the image of the body with the truth of individual identity. Not only are the urns identical, but the faces are almost entirely deprived of any animation or individual features. The very rigidity of the image, like the mirror reflection, therefore emphasizes its facticity, setting up a dynamic cycle of displacement. Rather than signifiers for an identity, presence or 'self', the link between signifier and signified, appearance and presence (despite the actual presence of the actors or actresses playing the figures) is disrupted:

> Concealing their bodies, effacing their faces . . . Beckett casts his actors as automata, sharply limiting the bodily expression that locates the actor's authorizing 'presence' within the performance. . . . instead of affirming a Stanislavskian 'I am,' their performance nearly reduces them to 'not I'.[12]

Because of this impassive and petrified appearance of the figures, 'being', presence or identity tend to be displaced from figure to voice, which, apart from the mouth, metonymically associated with the voice, is the only trace of animacy. Yet this animacy is also deceptive. The voices are monotone, regulated by the rhythm of the Light. Any 'natural' expressivity is subjected to this rapid, mechanical pace. The abstract quality of the voices was emphasized in a version of the play for BBC Radio 3 in which each voice was accompanied and regulated by a continuous sound of a different pitch, so that there was virtually no tonal variation and the voices sounded as devoid of individual 'expression' as the monotonous sounds which accompanied them.[13] The repetition of the entire play dissociates the figures' utterances from the concept of an animating central presence or 'I' which, on the model of the Logos, continually discloses itself through its utterances. The disruption of subjectivity is rendered even more complex by the dominant role played by the Light.

Although the heads fixed in their urns remain completely immobile, the stability of the image is radically disrupted by the continual and rapid movement of the Light from one head to the next. This movement draws attention to the division within the stage space between the figures and the Light, paralleling Lacan's division between the imago-perceived and the subject-perceiver. The second section of the text, termed 'The Meditation' according to Martin Esslin, in contrast to the Narration section[14] where the figures relate the story of their interconnected pasts, focuses on the relation between figures and Light and imputes the *need* to continue uttering to the tyrannical imperative of the Light:

20

W1: Bite off my tongue and swallow it? Spit it out? Would
that placate you?

(p. 154)

The focus therefore shifts from the figures' act of narration or
confession to the Light's act of extracting the narrations and to
its apparent function of revealing and judging the 'truth':

W1: Is it that I do not tell the truth, is that it, that some
day somehow I may tell the truth at last and then no
more light at last, for the truth.

(p. 153)

This emphasis on disclosure associates the act of seeing or
uncovering with the traditional concept of *aletheia* where truth or
presence, which cannot be directly perceived, *reveals* itself through
appearance. Beckett's use of the shifting spotlight can therefore be
seen as a parody of the association of light with the revelation
or appearance of presence and the disclosure of truth. In *Play*,
appearance, continually on the point of disappearance, reveals only
its opaque if tenuous surface rather than any inner essence or
truth. The strategies of representation, rather than producing
knowledge, truth and enlightenment, are revealed as arbitrary
mechanisms of discipline and control.

While the dynamic scenic text in *Play* prevents any integral
perception of the appearance or imago of the self, the characters'
monologues within the Narration section attempt to embody and
unify the temporal existence of the self into a coherent narrative
or history. Indeed, towards the end of the Meditation section, the
perception of the narrative seems to be identified with the perception of the figure's appearance, and offered as an *image* or completed object to be 'seen' by the Light:

W1: Yes, and the whole thing there, all there, staring you
in the face. You'll see it. Get off me. Or weary.
Spot from W1 to M.
M: And now that you are . . . mere eye. Just looking. At
my face. On and off.

(p. 157)

The play therefore seems to explore the connections between narrative, specularity and the desire for (self)mastery. Derrida sees in
narrative the ultimate authoritative (authoritarian) genre:

The narratorial voice is the voice of a subject recounting something, remembering an event or a historical sequence, knowing who he is, where [he] is, and what [he] is talking about. It responds to some 'police,' a force of order or law ('What "exactly" are you talking about?': the truth of equivalence). In this sense, all organized narration is 'a matter for the police,' even before its genre (mystery novel, cop story) has been determined.[15]

However, as the fragmented visual image, vacillating between appearance and disappearance, in fact resists specular possession, the narrative order of the play is also subverted. As with the image, the text in Beckett's work is never entirely devoid of representative content, and the text of *Play* retells the sordid story of a typically bourgeois 'ménage à trois'. However, this 'story'[16] is undermined in various ways. Each figure speaks only when the spotlight prompts him/her, not in interaction with the others, of whom each appears to be oblivious. The 'story' told by the text is therefore uttered only in fragments. There is no chronological order in the figures' 'discourse' or relation of the narrative, so that the text shifts backwards and forwards in time, as well as from a narrative point of view, making it very difficult to piece together into a 'whole'.

Indeed, the repetition of the entire play, as well as Beckett's suggestion of a variation in the order of the Light's movements and a fading of its intensity during the replay, undermines the Light's apparent authority and emphasizes its subjection to the same inexorable cycles of repetition as the figures. If the Light is not only a figure of authority but an author-figure, it continually fails to make an ordered, meaningful narrative out of the fragmented phrases and images that inhabit its skull-place.

Indeed, the narrative also suffers occasionally from what Beckett might term internal 'dehiscence'. For example, in one of W2's speeches, the space–time borders as well as the visuality of the narrative are ruptured, giving way to what might be termed a semiotic rhythm, in which identities or borders (between life and death or between heaven and hell) break down:

W2: Fearing she was about to offer me violence I rang for Erskine and had her shown out. Her parting words as he could testify, if he is still living, and has not forgotten, *coming and going on the earth, letting people in, showing*

people out, were to the effect that she would settle my
hash.

(p. 149, my italics)

As Paul Lawley has pointed out, this passage is an adaption from
Job I, vii, where Satan replies to God's question 'whence comest
thou?': 'From going to and fro in the earth, and from walking up
and down in it.'[17] Lawley also points out that this passage is one
of many which question the border between the Narration and
Meditation sections, as the activity of coming and going, and that
of 'letting people in, showing people out', parallels that of the
Light. A similar rhythm is also found in the motion of the lawn-
mower outside W2's apartment, while M attempts to break with
her: 'a little rush then another' (p. 151). This repetitive movement
then re-emerges in the second section as the very rhythm of the
Light:

> W2: Like dragging a great roller, on a scorching day. The
> strain . . . to get it moving, momentum coming –
> *Spot off W2. Blackout. Three seconds. Spot on W2.*
> W2: Kill it and strain again.

(p. 155)

The borders between the Narrative, the Meditation and the
actual spatial context therefore become problematized, as the narrative becomes indistinguishable from the *activity* of narration, or
uttering. What is represented in the text is placed in the context
of the attempt to utter and hear or understand, just as the visual
image is placed in the context of its continual appearance and
disappearance. In each case the represented is 'put in process', or,
to exploit Kristeva's French word-play (le sujet en procès), on
trial.

The referential value of the verbal text is therefore increasingly
undermined, as the speech of the figures becomes materialized as
utterance. This materialization is partly due to the deliberate use
of dated conventions in the construction of the narrative. Plot,
character and dialogue are largely constructed from cliché, to such
an extent as to increase the opacity of the narrative:

> W1: Then I forgave him. To what will love not stoop! I
> suggested a little jaunt to celebrate, to the Riviera or
> our darling Grand Canary.

(p. 150)

23

Andrew Kennedy refers to Beckett's awareness of ' "the burden of the past" . . . the museum of styles as a mausoleum'. In each of Beckett's texts, he argues, 'a particular literary language is isolated or parodied: set in a dramatic frame wherein the process of decay may be perceived'.[18] George Devine, who worked with Beckett on the 1964 National Theatre production of *Play*, referred to the 'novelettish quality' and to the 'melodrama of the hell on earth'.[19] The narrative therefore appears as an assemblage of clichés, an exposition of language as corpse or tomb (mirroring Devine's comparison of the three faces to writing on a tombstone), rather than an account which revives or relives something that once 'actually' happened. This is stressed by the repetition of the entire play, where the narration is repeated verbatim, with only a few minor variations in the order of the text.

The text therefore becomes sound without meaning, as the image is increasingly seen as appearance without presence. The rapid tempo of the delivery of the text not only removes the expressivity of the voices, but makes any attempt to understand the representative content of the text even more difficult. Individual stories and thoughts are reduced to ' "things" that come out of their mouths'.[20] Lacanian desire, which at first seems to drive the cycles of narration and perception, is increasingly erased, leaving simply a chain of empty signifiers.[21] Beckett therefore both exploits the convention of the 'interior monologue', of the text betraying or disclosing the inner thoughts of the character, and also overturns it, questioning the very existence of interiority, which is seen simply as a construct of the clichés used by the characters. The hell of judgement and the search for meaning becomes a meaningless *play* or replay.

The repetition therefore also questions the nature of the relationship between figures and Light. Although the Light is represented as external to the figures, an instrument of torture or 'dental drill' according to George Devine, it may also be an externalization of an inner conflict between the rational mind and the disordered fragments of experience that reason attempts but fails to order. The power relations, which at first appear polarized, with the Light as torturer/tyrant, are displaced, as the polarities of internal and external, self and other, are challenged. Light, figures and audience are trapped in a theatrical machine which reproduces its visual and narrative fragments without hope of resolution.

The Light therefore appears not only as a paradigm of an

author, but as a paradigm of the audience, attempting to perceive the fragmentary figures and to piece together or interpret the narratives. However, while the play may appear to exploit traditional relations between audience and text, casting the audience in the role of consumer or voyeur (Devine noted 'Audience privileged/Actors tortured'), this relation of subject/other between audience and performance is undermined. Since the play resists perception and interpretation, the audience continually fails to perceive the play, and in particular, any *meaning* the play might have. Indeed, any such meaning therefore becomes imputed to the audience's own desire for clarity and the structures of authority. As William B. Worthen has pointed out, Beckett not only reduces the actors to mouthpieces, but reduces the audience to a role, thereby denying the supposedly privileged status of the audience:

> The proscenium arch draws its frame around the represented tableau, rather than around its medium, the actor. It isolates the principal 'enunciators' of the spectacle – actors and audience – from one another, sealing the actors 'in character' while allowing the spectators to play out a privileged self-presence in the silent 'public solitude' of the auditorium. . . . '*Repeat play*' involves the spectator in the act of theatre and particularly complicates the 'asubjectivity of total presence' implicitly endorsed by his apparent location outside the field of play. Like the returning spool, like a reflection in the mirror, and like language itself, '*Repeat play*' compels us to play ourselves as 'other'. To see the play through to its finish, we must engage the self that we project toward the play as absorbed in the functions of theatre.[22]

While the audience perceives the heads' subjection to the mechanisms of the Light, indeed to the mechanisms of theatre itself, they also become aware of their own entrapment within their role as spectators. The exploitation of the power relations inherent within the structures of theatre becomes the main focus of *Catastrophe*.

CATASTROPHE: THE BODY IN REPRESENTATION

Catastrophe was written in French in 1982, two decades after *Play*, though it has similarities with the radio play *Rough for Radio II*, written also in French in the early 1960s. While *Rockaby* and *Ohio Impromptu*, written previously to *Catastrophe*, presented the drive to representation as a source of comfort, both *Catastrophe* and Beckett's last play for the stage, *What Where*, written in 1983, return to and develop Beckett's preoccupation with questions of representation, authority and power. *Catastrophe* is set in a theatre and focuses on the preparation of an actor's body to represent an image of catastrophe which will be presented to an audience. It is dedicated to Vaclav Havel, who was a dissident writer incarcerated for his writings at the time Beckett was writing the play. This has contributed to *Catastrophe*'s reputation as Beckett's 'political' play. However, rather than constituting an exception, *Catastrophe* reveals the preoccupation with power in its relationship to representation which characterizes much of Beckett's work, and its implications therefore extend far beyond any specific political context. While the apparent hierarchy of power in *Play* is undermined through repetition, in *Catastrophe* both the Protagonist and the Assistant are subjected throughout the play to the artistic and political power of the Director.

Catastrophe, unlike most of Beckett's plays since *Happy Days*, opens to reveal the recognizable space of a stage, fully lit. This cold, exposed space, limited by clearly visible walls, contrasts with the enveloping dark which surrounds the image in most of the later plays and which constitutes a temporary refuge if not a final escape from the relentless repetition of word and gesture. In *Catastrophe*, however, the space offers neither refuge nor escape. It is a space where the powerless are subject to the surveillance of the powerful. Forced to keep silent rather than to give testimony, the central spectacle here is the speechless body of the Protagonist. While Hamm, Pozzo or the Light in *Play* are as dependent upon their 'slaves' as the latter are subjected to them, the Producer's use and abuse of power in *Catastrophe* is absolute and unmitigated, as he exhibits and exploits the body of his victim.

The bare space and the harsh lighting emphasize the contrast between the three figures on stage, highlighting their costume, pose, movement or lack of movement. This series of contrasts or juxtapositions, particularly between the Director and the Protagonist, establishes the central power dynamic of the play. The Director, swathed in furs, is seated in a chair, towards the front of the stage. His appearance and manner convey affluence and authority. Through the Assistant he controls the stage space and the reference to attending a caucus presents him as a figure of institutional authority. It also underlines his freedom to enter and leave the theatre at will. The Protagonist, by contrast, is restricted to the narrow limits of his plinth, and is forced to remain upright throughout the performance. His pose, head bowed, hands buried in his pockets, emphasizes his confinement. He is ironically named, as he initiates no action until the closing moments.

Although no direct physical torture is inflicted upon the Protagonist, his body is evidently subject to physical restrictions and exploitation. Foucault's analysis of the institutional use of discipline to control and subdue individuals, instead of the older form of punishment through torture, reveals certain strategies which are also central to the power dynamic of Beckett's play. First of all, the enforced isolation and restriction of bodies in space:

> Each individual has its own place; and each place its individual. . . . Disciplinary space tends to be divided into as many sections as there are bodies or elements to be distributed. . . . Its aim was to establish presences and absences, to know where and how to locate individuals, to set up useful communications, to interrupt others, to be able at each moment to supervise the conduct of each individual, to assess it, to judge it, to calculate its qualities or merits. It was a procedure therefore aimed at knowing, mastering, and using. Discipline organizes an analytical space.[23]

This association of the drive to knowledge with coercion exercised upon the individual body is of considerable relevance to Beckett's oeuvre. Foucault stresses the importance of the apparatus of surveillance in the discipline and subjection of individual bodies, an apparatus 'in which the techniques that make it possible to see induce effects of power and in which, conversely, the means of coercion make those on whom they are applied, clearly visible'.[24]

From the opening tableau of *Catastrophe*, the play indeed focuses on the act of looking and the power relations inherent in this act. The Producer and his Assistant subject the Protagonist to their gaze:

> *D. and A. contemplate P. Long pause.*

At this stage, the Protagonist, head bowed, directs no gaze of his own. He is perceived as an object of vision, not only by the Producer and Assistant, but by the audience (both the audience envisaged by the Producer and the actual audience of Beckett's play). The gaze of the audience is specifically referred to:

27

D: Why the plinth?
A: To let the stalls see the feet.

(p. 297)

The spectacle in preparation therefore consists of the revelation of
the body of the Protagonist as an image of human suffering, or
catastrophe. In *Catastrophe* the role of the verbal text is reduced,
in order to foreground the Protagonist's body, manipulated by the
Director, to produce precisely the effect he intends:

D: Good. There's our catastrophe. In the bag. Once more
   and I'm off.

(p. 300)

The transformation of the body into artistic material is emphasized
by the whitening of the Protagonist's body:

A: Like that cranium?
D: Needs whitening.

(p. 299)

This process of whitening is extended to all of the Protagonist's
visible flesh, substituting the artificial for the human or, according
to Peter Gidal, the 'natural':

The examples of 'the white' in various representational practices (writing, painting, theatre, film) are given not as anal-
ogies for something else, but as usages inscribed in the process of making, constructing, producing as *artifice*, as opposed
to experiencing 'what is' as natural.[25]

Catastrophe plays upon the audience's awareness of the body transformed into a sign, into material to be manipulated, disciplined,
shaped. The body in representation is reproduced as a conditioned
image in accordance with the dominant laws, while any attempt
on the part of the powerless to speak or gesture is repressed:

The imposed-upon body is captured and framed in representation. Representation is a coded scene, a framing and fetish-
izing of the body as a whole (an image-pose) or a part.[26]

The exercise of discipline through the enforced and exposed visibility of the body ensures 'the subjection of those who are perceived
as objects and the objectification of those who are subjected'.[27]
   Indeed, the entire play is geared towards the objectification of

the Protagonist. Placed upon a plinth, he remains virtually motion-
less throughout most of the play, more statue than human being.
Until the closing moments, only his trembling bears witness to his
humanity. The role of the text emphasizes the objectification or
dehumanization of the Protagonist. Language is here a commodity
of the powerful. It is used both to implement the authority of the
Director and to deny the subject any means of expression. Bert
O. States notices:

> an idiomatic strain consisting of slang or 'trade' language:
> *Step on it; No harm trying; Bless his heart; Every i dotted to death;
> Get going; Is Luke around?; Where do you think we are? In Pata-
> gonia?; In the bag; Lovely; Terrific! He'll have them on their feet.* . . . .
> It implies the security of class membership. To say 'Lovely,'
> or 'Terrific!' (at least here) is to be in possession of your
> world. . . . This barrage of clichés is not himself a cliché but
> an invincible institute.[28]

Almost all of the Director's utterances are commands for information or action:

> D: Light. (*A returns, relights the cigar, stands still. D. smokes.*)
> Good. Now let's have a look. (*A at a loss. Irritably.*) Get
> going. Lose that gown.

> > (p. 298)

The body of the Protagonist is not only presented as a visible
object, but as a scientific or clinical object. It is progressively
exposed and dissected: 'the skull', 'the hands', 'the cranium', 'the
toes', 'the shins'. The Assistant with her white coat and brisk
efficient movements and the Director's use of scientific or clinical
language underlines the collaboration of knowledge and power in
the achievement of control over individual bodies:

> The historical moment of the disciplines was the moment
> when an art of the human body was born, which was directed
> not only at the growth of its skills, nor at the intensification
> of its subjection, but at the formation of a relation that in
> the mechanism itself makes it more obedient as it becomes
> more useful, and conversely. What was then being formed
> was a policy of coercions that act upon the body, a calculated
> manipulation of its elements, its gestures, its behaviour. The

29

human body was entering a machinery of power that explores it, breaks it down and rearranges it.[29]

However, Beckett is not simply exposing the mechanics of power, but the ways in which these strategies function within and seem to be integral to the processes of representation. There are implicit references to the ultimate symbol of power in the Judaeo-Christian tradition, the Almighty Creator, the omnipotent *metteur en scène*. The Director's call for Light, as well as his shaping of the human figure, the Protagonist, stresses his function as Creator. Indeed, the Protagonist not only evokes the pathetic figure of Man, but the figure of Christ, offered up as sacrificial victim, the spectacle of his crucified body presented to the gaze of the multitude. This Creator, however, is not the bearer of grace and mercy, but a figure of judgement, discipline and punishment – authority on a decidedly patriarchal and logocentric model. At one point, the Director leaves the stage to view the spectacle from the stalls. He does not, however, enter the physical space of the auditorium, although he announces that he is in the stalls. All we hear is his voice. The relationship between the fictional and the actual theatres of the play is therefore problematized, but the authority of the Director is also emphasized and located specifically in the voice of the master.

At the same time, the figure of the Director carries authority on a more secular level. It underlines the predicament of the artist in an authoritarian régime, forced to be manipulated by the dominant discourse or to be silenced – the Assistant indeed suggests that the Protagonist be gagged. Yet Beckett seems also to be indicating the problematic nature of representation itself. While language and spectacle may be used to assume and maintain power, there is also a recognition that the dominant laws of representation inevitably involve relations of power, discipline and control. H. Porter Abbott argues that in *Catastrophe*, Beckett presents the struggle with order and structure as a paradigm of other forms of repression:

> The aesthetic and the political ... merge in the insight that the political will that seeks to constrain human life to an imagined social order, imprisoning or eliminating those uncontrollable elements that threaten that order, is rooted with the aesthetic will that seeks to dominate the human through formal representation.[30]

30

There is also a recognition of the tragic paradox of the Lacanian subject, trapped in the order of the Symbolic and condemned to have [his] experience misrepresented and misappropriated within that order. As the Lacanian subject's desire is only reflected in the sign system as the desire of the other, the representation of suffering in *Catastrophe* is purely masquerade. The Protagonist's subjective experience of suffering has no means of representation within this scene of mastery.

There is a certain self-referentiality about *Catastrophe*. The figure of the Protagonist, in his long robe and wide-brimmed hat, recalls other Beckettian figures, as in *Eh Joe*, *Ghost Trio* or *Ohio Impromptu*, and the final fade-down to focus in on the head alone, off-handedly produced by the technician, Luke, is similar to the ending of many of Beckett's plays. Beckett seems to be exploring or exposing the paradox of the use of impersonal discipline, objectivity and technology in the *mise en scène* of a spectacle which deals with one of the most intimate areas of human experience, that of suffering, as do his own texts. Indeed, the discipline exercised by the Producer is rivalled by the discipline exercised by Beckett in the *mise en scène* of his own work. In a recent newspaper article, one witness describes the actress preparing for a performance of *Not I*:

> She climbed on to the dais and sat in the chair into which she was then locked – her head clamped so that only the organs of speech could move, and an iron bar pinning her into position. I think her wrists were strapped down as well.[31]

In the attempt to represent powerlessness, Beckett as director finds himself reproducing the mechanisms of power which subject his characters and actors. Beckett's engagement with these questions of discipline and authority should perhaps be taken more account of in debates around his role as director of his own work.

Catastrophe indeed contrasts these two spaces: the space and spectacle of power and the repressed, unrepresented space of suffering. The role of the Assistant emphasizes this contrast. If the Producer and Protagonist establish the two poles of the stage space, the Assistant is the mediator who crosses the space between. During the play she is the only mobile element, apart from the Director's exit. She also occupies an ambiguous position in relation to the dynamics of power. She collaborates with the Producer in her treatment of the Protagonist as an object to be manipulated and displayed, but she seems much more aware than the Director of the possibility that this subjected body might find some form of utterance. She expresses a fear that he might attempt to speak and suggests that he be gagged. She is, moreover, a fellow-victim, also under the power of the Director, forced to obey his every command. However, while the Director leaves the stage to view the image from the auditorium, she is momentarily relieved of his surveillance and instinctively expresses her revulsion (and revolt) towards the Director as she frantically wipes his chair before collapsing into it.

This sudden expression of revolt prefigures the final gesture of the Protagonist and sets up an awareness of another (unseen) scene beyond the authority of the Director and whatever figures of power he represents. The finished spectacle as it will be presented to the audience is revealed and we hear the thunderous applause of the Director's audience. However, after having been subjected to the gaze of others throughout the play, the Protagonist finally raises his head (despite the Director's certainty that such a thing is unthinkable) and fixes the audience with a stare of his own, until the applause falters.

The final gesture focuses attention on the role of the audience in the play. The Director's audience, who applaud such a spectacle, are seen to be the dupes or 'slaves' of the Director, accepting his created image as a faithful representation of suffering and playing exactly the role he has constructed for them:

> D: Stop! [Pause.] Now . . . let 'em have it. [Fade-out of general light. Pause. Fade-out of light on body. Light on head alone. Long Pause.] Terrific! He'll have them on their feet. I can hear it from here.
>
> (p. 301)

This role, however, is also played by the 'real' audience of the play. This audience are, of course, likely to sympathize with the Protagonist, but, because the play foregrounds the power dynamic inherent in its own production, the audience are made uncomfortably aware of the ambiguity of their role. At the same time, the play emphasizes the extent to which they have been manipulated in order to fulfil that role, and have therefore also been subjected to the mechanisms of representation as spectacle. Yet the very interplay of gazes, where that of the audience is reflected in the gaze of the Director, especially when he announces he is going to observe the spectacle from the auditorium, the gaze of the Assistant and, finally, the defiant gaze of the Protagonist, when, against all expectations, he raises his head and returns the audience's gaze, both exposes and deflects the gaze of power. Barbara Freedman sees such a deflection of the gaze as an important strategy in theatre's power to disrupt the frames of representation:

> Theatre is fascinated by the return of one's look as a displacing gaze that redefines as it undermines identity. The spectatorial gaze takes the bait and stakes its claim to a resting place in the field of vision that beckons it – only to have its gaze fractured, its look stared down by a series of gazes which challenge the place of the look and expose it as in turn defined by the other.[32]

Through the power of the look, the subjected body in *Catastrophe* becomes a resisting body, while the play as a whole exposes the apparatus of spectacle in its collusion with forces of authority and subjection. The play therefore underlines the faith in the need to 'go on', to bear witness to the traces of being which survive the repressive forces which humanity is 'heir to', underlying all of Beckett's work. This struggle suggests the ambiguity of Beckett's relation to humanism. Such a universalizing perspective may neglect the importance of specific context emphasized by contemporary cultural studies, but Beckett's work is nevertheless saturated with a sense of the suffocating weight of the historical, philosophical and literary heritage which continues to dominate and repress the articulation of difference. His work therefore relentlessly attacks the authoritarian structures and values inherited from post-Enlightenment humanism, but also seeks to keep faith with certain fundamental values invested in the humanist project. Herbert Blau suggests that Beckett's significance for contemporary experimental performers lies precisely in his refusal to forget or ignore the tarnished legacy of 'the old humanistic terms'.[33]

WHAT WHERE: SHADES OF AUTHORITY

As with many of the plays that Beckett has personally directed, although perhaps more than most, *What Where* became the object of continued modification and underwent a series of transformations during its passage from stage to television screen and back to the stage. The world première of the play was directed by Alan Schneider at the Harold Clurman Theatre, New York, in 1983.

Despite his well-known aversion to mixing genres, Beckett then adapted *What Where* for German television in 1985, working as usual with Süddeutscher Rundfunk. For this adaptation a number of significant changes were made both to the text and to the stage directions. These revisions in turn influenced the French production of the play by Pierre Chabert in April 1986 at the Petit Rond-Point, Paris, and the revised English text used by Stan Gontarski for his production at the Magic Theatre in San Francisco in 1987.

According to Jim Lewis, Beckett showed an uncharacteristic flexibility and openness to experiment during the production period of *Was Wo*:

> If you want to compare this production with all the others for television, there's one major difference. And that is that his concept was not set. He changed and changed and changed.[34]

The nature of the space, as well as the wider implications of the action, were changed during the process of adaptation for the 'small screen'. A consideration of this process is useful for the perspectives it sheds on *What Where* and on Beckett's use of the television medium. The late plays were undoubtedly influenced by Beckett's work for television, and *What Where* in particular recalls the recurring pattern in *Ghost Trio* and . . . *but the clouds* . . . where a scenario is imagined, revised and repeated by a controlling figure or voice.

The possibilities of control and discipline within the television medium are foregrounded within the verbal and visual text of *Ghost Trio* and . . . *but the clouds* . . . , yet the plays also draw attention to that which eludes the strict repetitive pattern of the structure. In the television version of *What Where*, Beckett uses technology as the agent of control over the bodies of the players, while in the stage version, the emphasis falls more on the physical subjection of each figure to the other. In both cases, the structure of repetition emerges as a cycle of interrogation which continually fails to capture presence and truth in either image or text.

There are several levels of repetition and reproduction within the structure of *What Where*: the repetition of figures or faces paralleled by the repetition of names, Bam/Bem/Bim/Bom; the reproduction of Bam himself, both V. in the outer space of the stage or screen and one of the actants within the playing area; the repetitious cycles of action and dialogue. Gilles Deleuze, in *Différence et Répétition*, sees the modern concern with repetition, which 'can be traced back to the works of Nietzsche, as founded upon the perception of a lack of original unity, the substitution of the play of difference for identity. The Platonic concept of representation or repetition as the copy of an original model gives way to the reproduction of copies, 'simulacres':

> Simulacra are systems in which different things are related to each other simply *by difference* itself. The essential thing is that in such systems there is no *preexisting identity*, no *interior resemblance* to be found. There is nothing but difference in the series, and difference of difference in the communication of the series.[35]

In *What Where* the division of the stage or screen space associates the pattern of repetition with the function of imagining. If, according to Gilles Deleuze, repetition is associated with the replacement of identity with difference, Beckett's work emphasizes that the process of imagining, linked with that of memory, ruptures space. Scenes are constructed and performed in a number of different stagings.

Samuel Taylor Coleridge envisaged Imagination as 'the living power and prime Agent of all human perception, and as a repetition in the finite mind of the eternal act of creation in the infinite I AM'.[36] However, Edward Casey has argued that the faculty of imagination in the finite mind is more concerned with absence than with the celebration of unquestioned presence affirmed in the pronouncement 'I AM':

> What the mind brings before itself in imagining is strikingly insubstantial. The re-creation is only of a pure possibility – ie., of a possibility *qua* possibility, not as would-be reality. Being purely possible, what we imagine is characteristically evanescent: hence our propensity to describe it as 'elusive' and 'fleeting.' When unsupported by objective structures, imaginings become phantomlike, streaking across consciousness like disembodied ghosts.[37]

Casey distinguishes between the substance of empirical reality and these illusory forms which are '*phenomenal* in character, a sheer appearing from which the brute presence of the empirically real

35

has been excluded'.[38] Such semblances must therefore be given substance through formal repetition:

> Only by successive re-creation can imagined content be maintained in mind and thus acquire continuity and cohesiveness. Without repetition such content collapses into a mere congeries of fragmented forms.[39]

Repetition can therefore be a means of 'presentifying' or bestowing presence upon the illusory ghosts of the imagination, but this presence in turn is merely phenomenal and dependent upon the process of repetition; it 'is not only indefinitely repeatable, but such as to *demand repetition*'.[40]

Beckett's work does portray the attempt to fix or capture presence through the repetition of image, movement or narrative. However, the emphasis on the act of repetition as well as the division of voice and figure, and in *What Where* the division of space, highlights the illusory, tenuous quality of these phantoms of the mind and focuses not primarily on what is imagined, but on the process of imagining and perceiving, the attempt rather than the ability to embody presence. Hence the divorce or difference between perceiver and perceived is both foregrounded and perpetuated. However, the distinction which Casey seems to assume between the space of the 'empirically real', which presumably includes the imaginer, and the insubstantiality of the imagined or the signifier is questioned in Beckett's work by the inclusion of the imaginer within the representative process: the deviser devised. While maintaining difference, Beckett not only questions the distinction between original and copy (since he breaks down the mimetic relationship between the image and the reality or presence it is supposed to imitate or reveal), but undermines the status of the author as creator, who, instead of controlling the mechanism of creation from the vantage point of an ontologically secure space, is himself caught up in the process of repetition, a finite and parodic imitation/imitator of the infinite I AM.

Beckett therefore replaces the notion of a homogenous space of presence with a shifting, dynamic space or series of spaces created through the play of difference and repetition. In *What Where* the way in which V. is visually represented contributes to the destabilization of space and identity. In the initial stage version, V. was signified by a megaphone, suggesting, as Martha Fehsenfeld has noted, something between the animate and the inanimate. In

36

relation to *Krapp's Last Tape*, Steven Connor argues that Beckett uses technological methods of voice reproduction to undermine the identification of speech with presence:

> *Krapp's Last Tape* moves to dissolve or undermine the dramatic qualities most commonly associated with speech – immediacy, originality and continuity. Crucial to this, as we have seen, are the physical materials necessary for the reproduction of language: the book, the envelope, the tape-recorder. These articles are simultaneously the means for preserving language and the means by which meanings in language are decoyed into new contexts.[41]

The use of a light to signify V. in the French stage version both maintains the technological quality (light is the medium whereby any form is rendered visible in the theatre) and also, through its biblical connotations, parodies the omnipotent presence of the Creator of Genesis.

The dynamic structure of the play, where space and process seem inextricable, is also dependent upon the ambiguity of the relationship between V. and the playing area. In the initial stage directions, the area seems both linked to V.'s consciousness and yet constitutes a separate space: both are lit separately and surrounded by space. The playing area therefore imitates an external zone, in which the figures physically move, as well as the internal space of memory or imagination. Indeed, the entrances and exits of the featureless cloaked figures in alternating poses of head bowed and haught suggests a multiplication of space, as a further space is created adjacent to the playing area, where the unseen but central action of the players – the interrogation of the figures in turn – takes place. The continual repetition of the movements also creates a time span beyond the individual, a perspective which in its concentrated minimalism seems to re-enact human history as a Nietzschean eternal repetition of cycles of domination and submission.

In the television version of *What Where*, however, this perspective of history and indeed power is reduced, as the space of the action is related more closely to the internal space of consciousness or memory. At the same time, the artificial nature of the television space emphasizes the illusory, simulated and parodic nature of creation according to Bam. Indeed, the synthetic quality of the television image seems to have fascinated Beckett. It appears to

37

lend itself more easily than the stage to the depiction of an imagined, constructed space. The flatter space, the smaller dimensions of the screen and the greater technological control over image and text can be used to create an image which is recognizable as a human figure or an interior, yet is also highly stylized and abstracted, as in *Ghost Trio*, with its geometrical visual patterns, or . . . *but the clouds* . . . where the body of the imaginer is perceived initially as a pattern of shadows. Beckett takes our most familiar visual images, whether the human body or a simple interior, and defamiliarizes them, breaking down the elements of body or room and reconstructing them as visual material to be manipulated by a 'controller'.

While these strategies introduce distance, television can also be used to interiorize the image, particularly in the use of close-ups, which Beckett particularly exploited in his first television play *Eh Joe*. This dual sense of interiority and distance is also due to the presence of the camera which Beckett frequently draws attention to as an active agent of perception. This is reinforced through foregrounding the reciprocal activities of showing and looking. Here, the look is used in order to achieve specular possession of the self, rather than to subdue the other (as in *Catastrophe*). However, the control supposedly offered by the look, and heightened by Beckett's use of the television medium, is at best, illusory. The images have to be repeated, and indeed draw attention to their own provisionality, their barely disguised screening of lack and absence. Both *Ghost Trio* and . . . *but the clouds* . . . are structured around the absence of a beloved other. In . . . *but the clouds* . . . this absence is figured by the shadowy face of a woman, which sometimes appears but more often does not. In *Ghost Trio* there is a contrast between the visual focus on the room and the figure within it, and the emotional loss presented through the non-visual medium of music. Repetition therefore emphasizes the persistence of desire which continually exceeds its expression and draws attention to the insubstantiality of these 'phantoms of the mind' which have continually to be 'represented'. These elements are central to the television version of *What Where*.

In the notebook Beckett prepared prior to the studio production of the television version of *Was Wo* the first change that he envisaged was the elimination of the figures, which are replaced by close-ups of the faces of the players:

Bodies + movement eliminated.
Faces only
Full face throughout[42]

The space therefore becomes much flatter, losing the depth and volume of the stage space. The play also becomes much more static, as the repeated exits and entrances are replaced by fade-ups and fade-outs. The alternation between head bowed and head haught is replaced by the eyes which are either open or closed. At first, the spaces inhabited by V./ S.(Stimm) and the players were to be differentiated by the lighting, although not so sharply as on stage:

> No further need of shadow
> surrounding P.A. 3/4
> of screen (P. A.) dimly lit
> Remainder in dark except
> for S. spot lit throughout[43]

During production, however, Beckett also eliminated the lit playing area, so that the background space inhabited by V. and the players is no longer distinguished. From being a space poised between an external space of oppression and submission, reminiscent of *Catastrophe*, and the inner space of consciousness, the space in *Was Wo* becomes apparently more internalized. Yet it is this spacing which subverts the notion of a closed or unified internal space. Such an operation:

> does not plant the theater inside the enclosure of a mental hideaway nor reduce space itself to the imaginary. On the contrary, in *inserting* a sort of spacing into interiority, it no longer allows the inside to close upon itself or be identified with itself.[44]

The intimacy of the television space is also countered by the emphasis on the image, on visual surface. This is particularly true of V., now represented also by a face. The undermining of the presence or immediacy of V. is conveyed in the television medium through extreme distortion of the face, using a mirror image, diffused even further through the use of an old warped pane of glass.[45] The visual distinction between V. and the players is retained as the image of V. is much larger, more diffuse and more faintly lit than the faces of the players. The stage directions emphasize that the four players should be as alike as possible, conveyed in the stage version through shrouding the figures in long, identical cloaks. During the television production, the individual features of each actor's face were minimized through control of the image, as Jim Lewis explained to Martha Fehsenfeld:

> We faded the smaller images in and out. I cut a small hole, an aperture, in a piece of cardboard, and placed each cardboard in front of each camera. We used four cameras at the same time, and we lined the aperture up to fit the face, the physiognomy of each face, because they weren't that much alike. He wanted them as alike as possible. We couldn't get that exactly but the apertures helped increase the similarity. Then we did make-up, rounding out the head, getting rid of the hair, the ears, darkening the outline to recede into black, hooded the faces. It looked like a science fiction sort of thing.[46]

Likewise, the voices are distorted, to achieve a distance from the identity of natural speech:

> Beckett had a struggle to achieve the Voice for example, this remote somewhat mechanical effect he wanted. We went through various phases. . . . [The actor] spoke relatively normally into the mike and it was stretched, made technically slower by the sound man, with further manipulation to avoid too much darkness in the voice.[47]

Both players and V. are therefore divorced from individual identities, becoming repetitions or reproductions of each other. The play of difference replaces a unified concept of self, the repetition of 'simulacres' for the reproduction of an original and originating presence. Creation and imagination or what is left of imagination seem to be reduced to the re-enactment of an endless masquerade.

Beckett's use of repetition therefore questions the very notion of identity and presence, both in relation to the dialectic presence/absence and in relation to the dialectic present/past or future:

> V: We are the last five.
>   In the present as were we still.

(p. 310)

What Where both presents the passage of time, 'Time passes', and yet, through repetition, not only of the action, but of the cycles of the seasons, from Spring through to Winter, undermines such a temporal hierarchy:

V: It is winter.
   Without journey.
   Time passes.
   That is all.

(p. 316)

The same denial of the presence of the present occurs in *Mimique*, the text by Mallarmé discussed by Derrida in 'The Double Session'. This text refers to a mime in which Pierrot 'murders' his wife through tickling her to death, and then commits suicide in the same way. The actor plays both man and wife, both perpetrator and victim. The 'murder' both takes place and does not take place, as the wife supposedly dies yet there is no physical violation of her body. The mimed death of Pierrot then reflects or repeats that of his wife. The action of the mime therefore sets up a dynamic fictional space which eludes fixed spatial or temporal boundaries, a 'between' space which Mallarmé called 'the hymen':

> The scene illustrates but the idea, not any actual action, in a hymen (out of which flows Dream) tainted with vice yet sacred, between desire and fulfilment, perpetration and remembrance: here anticipating, there recalling in the future, in the past, *under the false appearance of the present*. That is how the Mime operates, whose act is confined to a perpetual allusion without breaking the ice or the mirror: he thus sets up a pure medium, of fiction.[48]

The first presentation of the action in *What Where* is indeed as mime: action without words, a pure appearing (or rather reappearing, as the action is already presented as repetition). The same reappears as different, the present has already occurred and will be infinitely repeated. Thus, creation can be nothing other than memory, presented not as a voluntary faculty but rather as history, the inexorable process of eternal return:

> The world exists; it is not something that becomes, not something that passes away. Or rather: it becomes, it passes away, but it has never begun to become and it never ceased from passing away – it maintains itself in both. It lives on itself; its excrements are its food.[49]

41

Like the Opener in *Cascando*, V. can determine the opening or closing of 'play' but appears to have no control over what happens within the playing area. Beckett stressed this in the revised text, which removes the several interruptions by V. into the 'action', to replay it. Beckett noted in the Stuttgart production notebook: 'S. does not intervene in "action"'. Rather he suffers it passively, condemned to the same interminable pattern of repetition as the players, images of his image. The rhythm in *What Where* seems to emphasize this inexorability. There is very little variation, apart from the regular rise and fall of the interrogation passages. Each line is end-stopped, creating a rigid pattern of relentless and repeated monotony. Indeed, there seems to be no end to imagination, memory or repetition, to the recycling of the same or continually reduced material, even from beyond the grave. Beckett is said to have described the faces during the Stuttgart production as death masks.

The undermining of the hierarchical relation of presence/absence, original/copy, also implies a further polarity: that between truth and artifice or mask (truth and presence being twin hallmarks of ontological certainty). Derrida distinguishes two forms of mimesis: firstly, the presentation or unveiling of truth (aletheia), and secondly, the truthful (or false) imitation of 'what is':

> But in both cases, *mimesis* is lined up alongside truth: either it hinders the unveiling of the thing itself by substituting a copy or double for what is; or else it works in the service of truth through the double's resemblance (*homoiosis*). *Logos*, which is itself imitated by writing, only has value as truth.[50]

Such an interrogation is both presented and parodied in *What Where*. The dialogue centres on the absence of the text which would both reveal the truth and permit the construction of a narrative:

Bam: Well?
Bom: (*Head bowed throughout*) Nothing.
Bam: He didn't say anything?
Bom: No.
Bam: You gave him the works?
Bom: Yes.
Bam: And he didn't say anything?
Bom: No.

(p. 312)

42

It seems to be the absence of such a text which perpetuates the process of repetition and interrogation and maintains the dynamics of power. Throughout Beckett's work, the desire for truth is associated with the desire for mastery, involving the mechanisms of the master–slave dialectic. It is this aspect of *What Where*, most prominent in the initial stage version, which suggests that the play may be read not only as a parody of creation, but of history as a struggle for mastery over knowledge, or over meaning. Nietzsche wondered if the most powerful drive within the human race, capable even of pushing it to self-destruction, were not the will to truth:

> It may be that there remains one prodiguous idea which might be made to prevail over every other aspiration, which might overcome the most victorious: the idea of humanity sacrificing itself. . . . only the desire for truth, with its enormous prerogatives, could direct and sustain such a sacrifice.[51]

Beckett's work certainly seems to be haunted by the search for the 'key phrase' which will unveil truth, confirm presence or identity and release the victim from the endless cycle of repetition, as in *Play*, *Not I*, and indeed *Rough for Radio II*:

> A: It's hard on you, we know. You might prattle away to your latest breath and still the one . . . thing unsaid that can give you back your darling solitudes, we know. But this much is sure: the more you say the greater your chances.[52]

Failure to produce the necessary testimony leads to a perpetual sentence of torture (the torture consisting largely of the necessity to repeat). This is underlined in *How It Is*, where the text is inscribed or inflicted upon the body of the tortured by the torturer who is then in turn subjected to the text and tortured. Likewise, in *What Where* the first round of dialogue deals with the unnamed victim's inability or refusal to say what and where (the interrogation itself is reported not presented), but the subsequent repetitions place this report in the context of the cycles of torture inflicted upon the torturers who are accused of lying, of having heard the vital information but refusing to disclose it:

> Bam: It's a lie. [*Pause.*] He said where to you. [*Pause.*]

43

> Confess he said where to you. [*Pause.*] You'll be given
> the works until you confess.
>
> (p. 315)

Indeed, part of the impossibility of uncovering the true statement
is the fact that those who listen, record and indeed judge the
confession are completely ignorant of what it is they are looking
for, as in *Rough for Radio II*:

> A: Of course we do not know, any more than you, what
> exactly it is we are after, what sign or set of words.[53]

Likewise, the text of *What Where* focuses on the continual veiling
or deferral of truth, which perpetuates the series of interrogations.
Representation as mimesis (or mastery of truth) is both framed
and parodied: the action and dialogue within the playing area
refer mainly to the vain but unrelenting attempt to extract a
truthful text or confession, while this stage both frames the absent
space of interrogation and is itself framed by the space or spaces
of the play as a whole, where representation or creation is exposed
as an endless masquerade or parade of masks. The content of *What
Where*, as Peter Gidal has argued in relation to Beckett's plays in
general, does not present any meaning or truth, but rather reflects
back upon and exposes its own processes of representation:

> Content is not a stated concept... what is meant is that
> which makes and breaks meaning, not within but against.
> This posits neither transcendental nor transcendent possi-
> bilities, but the positioning of each moment in the history of
> its process.[54]

Indeed, the extraction of truth may refer not only to the process
of creation but to that of interpretation. The author not only
interrogates himself (or his own other(s)) as material for his fiction,
but the work is interrogated by its readers, critics or, in the case
of drama, directors, actors or reviewers. The play can therefore
also be seen as a parody of the author's, director's or indeed
critic's attempts to *interpret* or extract the truth from the writer's
work: the English text describes the process of torture as giving
him 'the works' and the French text uses the verb 'travailler' –
both suggesting enforced study sessions! The tyranny inherent in
the relationship between author and work, or critic and work, is
both exposed by the cycles of interrogation and challenged by the

44

de-hierarchization of the relations of power through the levelling effect of the pattern of repetition. The play closes (there is no suggestion of an end) with a denial, not only of the control and authority of authorship, but also of any predetermined meaning which might be forcibly extracted by spectators or critics:

> Make sense who may.
> I switch off.

> (p. 316)

The notion of the text as founded on the presence of truth in *What Where* is therefore replaced by the repetition of a process in which truth is endlessly displaced, leaving only the mechanical repetition of the pattern. At the same time, the rigidity of the pattern is countered by the spaces opened up by the operation of repetition (as difference), which undermines not only the hierarchical opposition between absence and presence, truth and mask, but that between form and space, between the visible and the invisible. Jim Lewis stressed in the interview with Martha Fehsenfeld that 'the players – those floating faces – weren't really there. . . . What you see is not there.'[55] The repetition or play of 'simulacres' not only destabilizes ontological certainties or hierarchies, but is also a means of foregrounding space itself, the unfigurable absence of centre or 'self' which challenges and redefines the limits of representation:

> This 'materialism of the idea' is nothing other than the staging, the theater, the visibility of nothing or of the self. It is a dramatisation which *illustrates nothing*, which illustrates *the nothing*, lights up a space, re-marks a spacing as a nothing, a blank: white as a yet unwritten page, blank as a difference between two lines. 'I am for – no illustration. . . .'[56]

The plays explored in this section therefore parody the association of mimesis with truth, presence and authority, while emphasizing that these structures and values continue to permeate Western representational systems. The plays considered in the next chapter, *That Time* and *A Piece of Monologue*, continue Beckett's preoccupation with authority, but shift from an investigation of authority as a will to power, discipline and knowledge to an exploration of the structures of authority within language. Both of these plays focus on individual subjectivities and the construction and undermining of identity in and through language.

2

MASQUERADES OF SELF

No longer the identification of our faint individuality with
the solid identities of the past, but our 'unrealisation' through
the excessive choice of identities. . . . Taking up these masks,
revitalizing the buffoonery of history, we adopt an identity
whose unreality surpasses that of God, who started the
charade.[1]

Did you ever say I to yourself in your life come on now.[2]

In *That Time* and *A Piece of Monologue*, Beckett continues his assault
on the structures of identity offered by the dominant forms of
representation. The texts of both plays exploit and subvert the
structures of monologue and autobiography which traditionally
support the concept of self-hood. While in many of the plays
considered so far, the forces of authority requesting evidence of
identity have been externalized, the struggle between the Symbolic
law and the subject's experience of lack and fragmentation is here
located more explicitly within an individual psyche. In *That Time*
and *A Piece of Monologue*, as in much of Beckett's late drama, this
struggle emerges through the interaction between the performative
subject who repeatedly attempts to articulate his/her experience
and the symbolized fragments of his/her existence. In particular,
both plays focus on the destabilization of the textual and visual
frames used to figure the subject and [his] history.

Barbara Freedman notes that 'theatre refers both to a framed
product and to the acts of framing and staging'.[3] Beckett's late
theatre exploits this ambiguity. In *That Time* and *A Piece of Monologue*, the excessive rhythm of *Not I*, where a large proportion of
the text is lost through the speed of delivery, is replaced by the
intensity of perceiving the fragmented images and scenes of the

46

text itself. Yet, within the text, the focus shifts from the narrative or descriptive content to the process of staging the self before the (other) self as audience. These plays therefore recall the psycho-analytic drama where the image (and later the name) of the self are assumed under the spectatorship of the Mother. Here, how-ever, the relation to the other has been lost: Mother and friends in *That Time*; all the 'loved ones' in *A Piece of Monologue*. According to Judith Butler, narrative or fiction, 'in which "I" am the origin of a fictive otherness',[4] stands in 'for the real others who have been lost in the process'.[5] *That Time* and *A Piece of Monologue* replace the look of the lost (M)other[6] with a dispersed and decentred perceptual function (in which the audience is impli-cated) which questions the customary borders of the 'self' and reinforces the alienation of the subject from authorized forms of identity and self-hood. The plays present a contrast between the repeated attempts to produce, frame and perceive a visual image or narrative of the subject's existence, or lack of existence, and the dissolution of all stable frames and representations in silence or the word-flow of utterance.

In their treatment of Time and identity, these plays both chal-lenge the individual borders of identity and shift between the time perspective of the individual and that of human history. Indeed, these plays seem to imply a recognition of identity as a series of masks, as the representation of 'self' becomes the reproduction of a series of interchangeable images of existence. The questioning of identity and origins in these plays recalls Nietzsche's challenging of the concept of history as the pursuit of the origin, which he replaces with that of genealogy. According to Michel Foucault's reading of Nietzsche, the genealogist 'will push the masquerade to its limit and prepare the great carnival of Time where masks are constantly reappearing'.[7] Yet both plays also anticipate the possibility of escaping the relentless cycles of existence and the depiction of that existence, through the production of images or narratives of ending where the remaining visual and verbal forms transform themselves into darkness and silence.

That Time and *A Piece of Monologue* reduce theatre to the point where it hardly seems to be taking place at all. According to James Knowlson, 'Beckett was very much aware that *That Time* lay "on the very edge of what was possible in the theatre" '.[8] Yet, through the juxtaposition of scenic and textual forms and spaces, there is a constant evolution in the perception of what is being represented,

47

as the categories of space and time, past and present, external and internal, absence and presence, identity and difference are undermined. Any mobility in the plays lies therefore in the shifting perspectives within the perception of stage and text. As Stanton B. Garner argues:

> It is Beckett's genius in his later plays to explore the activity lodged within stillness and to sound the depths of visual latency. The result . . . is to etch the contours of performance even more within the spectator and to replace a theater of activity with a theater of perception, guided by the eye and its efforts to see.[9]

THAT TIME: BETWEEN FRAMES

As in *Not I*, fragmentation and juxtaposition characterize the stage image of *That Time*, where all forms, visual or aural, are isolated from each other and surrounded by space. The only visual material is the image of the head of the Listener, situated just off centre stage, separated spatially both from the absent body and from the text which is in turn fragmented into three disembodied and recorded voices, issuing from loudspeakers to the left, centre and right of the stage. The image of the Listener therefore focuses on the function of perceiving, although utterance and perception are interdependent in both plays, as they are in almost all of Beckett's dramatic works. Instead of the non-specular image of the mouth which tends to dominate the dimly lit image of the Auditor in *Not I*, the spectators are presented with the spotlit head of a white-haired old man. The only movement of the head, until the end, is the opening and closing of the eyes, which highlights the activity of perception. Yet what the head 'sees' is the spoken text – the process of seeing is transformed into that of listening, and vice versa.

The voice is therefore entirely dissociated from the body, yet it dominates the stage space, as it issues from three speakers situated at each side and at the centre of the scenic space. Whereas the text of *Play* and *Not I* is submitted to an unnaturally rapid pace, so that the dynamic stage image tends to dominate the content of the text, in *That Time*, for the most part, there is little but the spoken text to maintain the audience's attention. A space which is usually associated with the visual is dominated by the verbal,

48

the mimetic by the diegetic. Yet precisely because of the lack of visual scenic material the faculty of seeing, both that of the Listener and that of the audience, shifts from the outer 'eye of the flesh' to the inner eye of the imagination. The audience's imagination becomes the scene where the Listener's memories are staged. The two categories of perception, external or physical and internal or imaginative, are thereby juxtaposed.

The separation of the head from the three voices external to it emphasizes the ambiguity of the stage space. The visual image of the head seems to suggest an external view of an old man on his death bed: 'Old white face, long flaring white hair as if seen from above outspread' (p. 228). Yet the haunting quality of the spotlit image, the pale skin and the long white hair, as well as the position of the disembodied head, situated unnaturally three metres above stage level and seen as if from above, has a disorienting effect upon the spectator,[10] preventing him or her from perceiving the stage space as a naturalistic death-bed scene. As the Listener closes his eyes to listen to the voices, he seems to be retreating into an inner world. While the voices appear to occupy a space that is external to the head, this space can also be seen as an externalization of the inner space of the Listener's mind or memory. The impression of internality, even of intimacy, is reinforced through the sound of the breathing which is heard before the voices begin. When David Warrilow played the role of the Listener at the Théâtre Gérard Philippe in 1983, the breathing was intensely physical, laboured, with every catch in the throat registered. This tended to transform the space into an internal cavern which threatened to engulf auditorium and stage, conflicting with the external perspective offered by the head.

The absence of body, apart from the head, and any other scenic information means that, as in *Not I*, images or memories of body and world are produced solely through the text. While the stage image stresses the 'here and now' of the speaker's voices relayed to him across the stage space, the text recreates other spaces and other times, opening up a vast perspective of the history of an individual from birth to old age and even beyond, to encompass the history of the human race according to Christianity, through the references to Adam and Eve, or indeed to preceding civilizations: 'perhaps way back in childhood or the womb worst of all or that old Chinaman long before Christ born with long white hair' (p. 230). Such a multiplicity of identities recalls Nietzsche's parade of historical masks. Yet this immense perspective is telescoped into the stage present, as the image of an old man with long white hair referred to in the text parallels the stage image of the Listener. Since the old Chinese man has just been born while the Listener is on his death-bed, the juxtaposition not only superimposes past and present, but death and birth, in a pattern that is repeated throughout *That Time*, where the interplay between identity and difference simultaneously posits and demolishes the spatial and temporal categorization of experience.

The only access to history or memory that Beckett's characters have is through language. For the characters of Beckett's late plays, language appears to give access both to the variety of forms, spaces and light of the external world, absent from the darkness of the stage present, and to the accumulated knowledge or memories of the past, whether their own past or that of a civilization. Yet this past can be seen simply as a function or a construct of the language system, preserved in the pages of dusty tomes in public libraries or deployed in the present moment of utterance. History and memory are presented both as a means of restoring the past and as the collected debris of the present, emphasized by one of the images in voice B of a dead rat floating down a river.

In *Proust*, Beckett quotes the author of *A la recherche du temps perdu* who insists that true possession of the other (or of the self) is dependent on possession of their entire history, the merging of discrete spatial and temporal moments of a life into a homogeneous whole:

> We imagine that the object of our desire is a being that can be laid down before us, enclosed within a body. Alas! it is the extension of that being to all the points of space and time that it has occupied and will occupy. If we do not possess contact with such a place and with such an hour we do not possess that being.[11]

Yet, as the author of *Proust* emphasizes, such an ideal is impossible to achieve since 'all that is realised in Time (all Time produce), whether in Art or Life, can only be possessed successively, by a series of partial annexations – and never integrally and at once'.[12] Hence the narration of the protagonist's past is splintered into the three separate voices, each dealing with a different period in the Listener's life. According to Walter Asmus' report, Beckett specified that B is the young man, A the middle-aged man and C the old man.[13] Moreover, each period is not narrated continuously, but is broken into fragments, intercut by the fragments of the other two periods. Memory, inscribed in language, therefore produces a myriad of times, spaces and identities, transforming the space of the stage into a space animated and ruptured by temporal differences, while such temporal differences are presented on stage as spatial discontinuity. The reassuring 'wholeness' or fixity of the stage space as stable visual ground is disrupted.

The attempt to possess or perceive also ironically creates another level of difference – between the subject and the representations of his own existence in language, questioning the illusion of unity and identity suggested by the pronoun 'I': 'did you ever say I to yourself in your life come on now' (p. 230). This alienation or divorce is indicated within the text – where the subject is referred to as 'you', creating a difference between the enunciating or narrating subject and the subject or persona of the narrative – and on stage through the separation of voice(s) from listener. The stage image therefore concretizes in spatial terms the divisions between listener-perceiver, voice and textual persona(s), while the spatial and temporal fragmentation of the text emphasizes the lack of continuity between the fragments which constitute the representation of the old man's life-history. The interplay between head and voices and between the various fragments of the text thus prevents the audience from locating any stable, unified centre of subjectivity in the play.

Yet the dynamic of the play consists not only in the contrast between these spaces, times and selves, but in the glimpses of identity or continuity. While the head and the voices are separated across the stage space, the use of the second person, as in Beckett's prose text *Company*, rather than the third, as in *Not I*, creates an intense relationship between them and also suggests an identity between the head and the various incarnations of the protagonist within the text. Moreover, while the voices are differentiated and fragmented, the text emphasizes that they are all 'moments of one and the same voice' (p. 227). While the voices are spatially fragmented, apart from two short intervals, the verbal flow is itself uninterrupted: the moments 'relay one another without solution of continuity'.

The same balancing of continuity and contrast is characteristic of the relationship between the textual fragments. Beckett's use of juxtaposition within the stage or textual space is paralleled by his

51

use of repetition within the text, where similar phrases and images are repeated between different voices, sections or instalments, questioning the apparent distinctions between the voices. Moreover, the different times and spaces evoked in the text are not only compared and contrasted amongst themselves, but are contrasted with moments when the divisions of chronology or of geographical location dissolve. The play of difference and identity through juxtaposition and repetition is therefore closely related to the questioning of traditional categories of space (internal or external, bounded or unbounded) and time (past or present, finite or infinite).

Gérard Genette distinguishes three modes of *récit*, or narrative, which relate to the categories of space and time, internal and external. The first two are *narration* and *description*, both of which tend to refer to experiences of the protagonist in the external world. Narration, however, tends to deal with the succession of events in time, while description is more static, fixing the objects described in space:

> Narration restores, in the temporal succession of its discourse, the equally temporal succession of events, whereas discourse must modulate, in discursive succession, the representation of objects that are simultaneous and juxtaposed in space.[14]

Genette's third category of *récit*, is termed *discourse*. The other two modes both have a certain visual reference, even the narration. The third, however, deals with the internal activity or functioning of the production of discourse. Whereas the first two describe external events or scenes, the third is concerned with the subject in its relation to language: ' "subjective discourse" is that in which, explicitly or not, the presence of (or reference to) I is marked, but this is not defined in any other way except as the person who is speaking this discourse.'[15] Genette's first two categories seem to correspond in *That Time* to passages of movement and description in the *récit* of the protagonist's past, and the third to the regular breaks in the narration, particularly the repeated phrase 'when was that' which returns the focus to the moment of utterance or enunciation, as in the following passage:

> A: straight up the rise from the wharf to the high street and there not a wire to be seen only the old rails all rust when was that.

(p.229)

The text also shifts from image or narrative to the reporting of speech production:

> A: or talking to yourself who else out loud imaginary conver-
> sation there was childhood for you ten or eleven on a
> stone among the giant nettles making it up now one voice
> now another till you were hoarse and they all sounded
> the same.

(p. 230)

That Time continually shifts from the narrative to the descriptive mode – from an emphasis on movement and the passing of time to moments of description usually associated with an object or objects, when time seems to have been temporarily halted. Yet if these modes can be identified in Beckett's text, their differentiation also serves to highlight their interpenetration. The stillness of description is interrupted by the impossibility of arresting motion, either that of the body or that of time, while the experience of time is frequently presented in terms of spatial difference. Beckett therefore exploits these two modes, yet also confuses them, so that if time is spatialized, space is also infused with time.

Mikhail Bakhtin has written of this interlinking of space and time in literature under the category of 'chronotopes': 'We will give the name *chronotope* (literally, "time space") to the intrinsic connectedness of temporal and spatial relationships that are expressed in literature.'[16] Bakhtin deals mainly with the literature of antiquity and ends with a discussion of Rabelais. He emphasizes the dominance of exteriority in this literature, the lack of distinction between the private and the public:

> The square in earlier (ancient) times itself constituted a state
> (and more – it constituted the entire state apparatus, with
> all its official organs), it was the highest court, the whole of
> science, the whole of art, the entire people participated in
> it. . . . And in this concrete and as it were all-encompassing
> chronotope, the laying bare and examination of a citizen's
> whole life was accomplished, and received its public and
> civic stamp of approval. . . . Here the individual is open on
> all sides, he is all surface, there is in him nothing that exists
> 'for his sake alone', nothing that could not be subject to
> public or state control and evaluation. Everything here, down
> to the last detail, is entirely public.[17]

53

However, Bakhtin also anticipates the fragmentation of chronotopes in modern literature, linking this development with the increasing emphasis on interiority, on the invisible and the unnamable:

> In following epochs, man's image was distorted by his increasing participation in the mute and invisible spheres of existence. He was literally drenched in muteness and invisibility. And with them entered loneliness. The personal and detached human being – 'the man who exists for himself' – lost the unity and wholeness that had been a product of his public origin. Once having lost the popular chronotope of the public square, his self-consciousness could not find an equally real, unified and whole chronotope; it therefore broke down and lost its integrity. . . . The human image became multi-layered, multi-faceted. A core and a shell, an inner and an outer, separated within it.[18]

The text of *That Time* seems to contrast two different types of chronotope: firstly, the external images and narratives of the life-history of the protagonist, and secondly, the non-visual internal space animated by discourse. This is also related to what might be called a third chronotope, the ideal yet terrifying 'boundless space . . . endless time' of absence or death, the 'ejaculation' which Beckett told Laurence Harvey 'would be the "most perfect form of being" if it could ever be achieved – the ideal absence in which every perception and memory will be "gone from mind" '.[19] It is, however, the very processes of perception and memory which maintain the dynamic by perpetuating the division between self and (other) self and between the subject and the representations of its body, world and history. Beckett's use of space in *That Time* emphasizes this fragmentation and division within the 'self', yet at the same time, through the juxtaposition of these fragments of differing spaces and times both within the text, and between text and stage, the boundaries between them continually shift and metamorphose one into the other. This ambiguity of difference and confusion relates both to a textual or dramatic practice of undermining stable conceptual and perceptual categories, and to a portrayal of subjectivity founded on a dynamic of desire which also defies stable positions of identity.

Voice A relates the middle-aged protagonist's journey back to the city of his birth (recognizable here as Dublin) in search of the ruin where he used to hide as a child, and therefore seems to privilege the narrative and factual, external mode. Yet Bakhtin emphasizes the inseparable link between the temporal and the spatial 'peregrinations' of the protagonist of Apuleian fiction: 'The most characteristic thing about this novel is the way it fuses the course of an individual's life (at its major turning points) with his actual spatial course or road – that is with his wanderings.'[20] Certainly, within *That Time* the interminable spatial trajectories of the body are linked with the protagonist's life-journey through Time. Indeed, the journey in *That Time* is also a journey through time, in the attempt to make contact with an earlier space, time and identity: 'that time you went back that last time to look was the ruin still there where you hid as a child' (p. 228). But this journey in search of a lost childhood is a failed one, as all means to reach the Folly, the goal of the protagonist's visit, are frustrated. The halting of the journey is underlined by the shift from narration of movement to description, particularly in section II, where the protagonist attempts to reach his destination by rail. The station proves not to be a stage on the way, but a terminus to his journey: 'so foot it up in the end to the station bowed half double get out to it that way all closed down and boarded up Doric terminus of the Great Southern and Eastern all closed down and the colonnade crumbling away' (p. 231). Yet these supposedly static descriptions, of the tram rails or of the railway station, or indeed of the childhood refuge, are descriptions of ruins, and are therefore impregnated with time and motion, evoking the same passage of time and processes of decay to which the protagonist and his 'loved ones' are also subject.

Voice B at first offers a striking contrast to the predominant images in the previous scenes. As James Knowlson indicates 'each of the three accounts is given its own physical setting, its own season of the year, even its own light, as well as its own range of incidents and images'.[21] In B's account, for the first time, there is sunlight instead of greyness. This *récit* is also predominantly in the descriptive mode: there is no action, and practically no movement. Instead of a town, the setting is the countryside: elemental, natural objects are evoked – the wood, the wheatfields and, of central importance, the stone. Moreover, the protagonist is not alone, but with a loved one. The figures are in harmony with their setting, indeed the universe, as the scene encompasses earth and sky, stretching tranquilly to the horizon: 'just there on the stone in the sun with the little wood behind gazing at the wheat or eyes closed all still no sign of life not a soul abroad no sound' (p. 228). Rather than a snatched moment of respite, all is stillness and calm. This is an image of harmony and complementarity between the two figures and between figures and ground. The stillness is broken only by the lover's vows or by the movement of their eyes, which, like those of the Listener, are either open or closed, but on sky rather than on darkness: 'blue dark blue dark'. However, the fact that the image is painted in words means that it has to be repeated constantly, as the words fade as soon as they are uttered and can never achieve the simultaneity of the visual object. As in Beckett's short prose piece *Still*, the same gesture is described again and again, but it is never captured, because stillness and simultaneity are incompatible with time as difference and motion.

Voice C also contrasts the narrative and description of specific external times and spaces with the dissolution of distinct categories. The setting is again a city, but this time recognizably London, contrasting with the cityscape of Voice A. This voice begins with a scene in the Portrait Gallery: 'that time in the Portrait Gallery in off the street out of the cold and rain slipped in when no-one was looking and through the rooms shivering and dripping till you found a seat marble slab and sat down to rest and dry off and on to hell out of there when was that' (p. 228). Rather than a contrast between child and mature man, the scene in the Portrait Gallery is juxtaposed with visits to other public places: the Public Library, the Post Office. Different times and visual environments are evoked and yet the descriptions mirror each other, balancing difference and identity. In each the relentlessness of motion is contrasted with a moment of stasis and snatched respite. These scenes therefore also recall the pattern of movement and stasis in the scenes of Voice A, despite the circumstantial differences of time and place. This confusion of disparate scenes is emphasized by the repetition of the same phrases from scene to scene. Like the old man, the child is longing to escape to the Folly 'slip off when no-one was looking' (p. 229). The questing protagonist in A also seeks temporary refuge on the slab of a doorstep 'for it to be time to get on the night ferry and on to hell out of there' (p. 232).

The supposedly external narration of specific occasions is also set against the interminable series of rainy winter days. Indeed, particular times, spaces and identities merge together into the fictional image of a formless, undifferentiated mass or mud in which the protagonist is entrenched: 'crawling about year after year sunk in your lifelong mess muttering to yourself who else you'll never be the same after this you were never the same after that' (p. 230). This dual perspective of, on the one hand, change or evolution associated with 'turning points' and, on the other, sameness, recurs throughout the text: 'always having turning points and never but the one the first and last that time curled up worm in slime when they lugged you out and wiped you off' (p. 230).

Beckett therefore increasingly blurs the distinction between external and internal, or rather subsumes all distinctions between the various representations of various existences within the text (or on stage), within the primary distinction between the formless subject and the various forms or representations in which, time after time, it attempts to be. The subject is differentiated and alienated from the skull enclosing it, from the words it utters or the memories or narratives it tells, from every form or representation of existence, unable to escape from or to identify with either the body or language: 'tottering and muttering all over the parish till the words dried up and the head dried up and the legs dried up whosever they were or it gave up whoever it was' (p. 232). In the face of such dispossession, memories, facts and fantasies become simply 'fodder' for the imagination hungry for images of existence, or else, of dissolution:

> dragging his hunger through the sky
> of my skull shell of sky and earth
> stooping to the prone who must
> soon take up their life and walk
> mocked by a tissue that may not serve
> till hunger earth and sky be offal[22]

That Time can therefore also be seen as animated by the dynamic of desire: the continual quest or physical displacement of the protagonist within the narrative, in search of the past or of refuge, mirrors the desire of the subject trapped in the masquerade of signifiers. The visuality of these scenes is emphasized. The drive towards specular fixity can therefore be linked with the desire for metaphysical and ontological certainty. While Beckett's texts testify to the intense desire to see/hear/possess images of existence, his subjects are deprived of any position of certainty, authority or possession, hence perpetuating the cycle of unfulfilled need/desire

mirrored in the relentless journeying of the narrative's protagon-
ist(s), the succession of images and the unceasing flow of speech
of the voices.

In the third section of Voice A, the identities of the two narrated
selves of the protagonist, the older man and the child, the white-
haired Listener and the voices on stage become blurred: the spatial
and temporal contexts and conditions are different and yet all three
identities merge in the emphasis on invention, on the production of
fictions/memories/speech: 'making it all up on the doorstep as you
went along making yourself all up again for the millionth time
forgetting it all where you were and what for' (p. 234). This shift
of emphasis from the content of the narrated scenes to the conditions of their perception or production is emphasized within the
first section of voice B, when there is a sudden shift from a focus
on the image itself to a focus on the space against which it is
framed. All times and spaces are engulfed or contained in this
indeterminate space–time of the mind, reversing the categories of
internal and external: 'one thing could ever bring tears till they
dried up altogether that thought when it came up among the
others floated up that scene' (p. 229). The ambiguity of the space
is emphasized through the juxtaposition of instalments where the
space described is sometimes the space of the mind and sometimes
the interior of a room, frequently used by Beckett as a space which
is simultaneously external and internal. The 'background' space
is therefore foregrounded and the focus shifts from the narratives
to the spatial frame into which they are inserted.

This space is not static, but is animated by the process of
perceiving and the desire for these images to relieve the darkness.
The tension 'outwards', the imaginative recreation of the external
world, is contrasted with the return to darkness. This image also
links text and stage spaces, as the audience also has been concen-
trating on the content of the images until the two intervals in the
text, where there is silence for three seconds and then breathing
for seven seconds before the voices resume, confronting the spectators with a silent, almost empty stage, apart of course, from the
Listener. The description within the text therefore acts as a 'mise
en abyme' for the performance as a whole, where the darkness of
the stage is relieved by the image of the head and the scenes related
by the voice, as the darkness of the protagonist's consciousness is
relieved by the remembered scenes.

Since the scenes appear as contained within the space–time of stage or skull, they appear not as recreations of a previous reality, but as concretizations of the void, shapes and sounds constructed from silence and darkness by the function of the imagination/ memory: 'hard to believe harder and harder to believe you ever told anyone you loved them or anyone you till just one of those things you kept making up to keep the void out just another of those old tales to keep the void from pouring in on top of you the shroud' (p. 230). As Stan Gontarski argues, 'We finally have, not the traditional truth/illusion dichotomy, but an interplay of illusions, of fictions, one fictive construct played against, balanced with, opposed to, in suspension with, embedded in another, one displacing and displaced by the other.'[23]

As the performance progresses, however, the void becomes more and more pervasive. The motion of Time and displacement, becomes, in Voice A, the anticipation of departure: 'till it was night and time to go till that time came' (p. 234). In Voice C, the visible world and the body of the old man progressively fade. The old man becomes almost invisible, others see through him while the scene in the Public Library literally disintegrates and 'returns' to dust: 'not a sound only the old breath and the leaves turning and then suddenly this dust whole place suddenly full of dust when you opened your eyes from floor to ceiling nothing only dust' (p. 235). In Voice B, the various scenes become increasingly indistinguishable as temporal categories merge: 'when was that an earlier time a later time before she came after she went or both' (p. 233). As in Voice C, the visual world, here announced as fictional or constructed, gradually fades: 'nothing stirring only the water and the sun going down till it went down and you vanished all vanished' (p. 233), until there are no more images and no more words, only empty space and silence, both without and within.

The dissolution of the images within the text is paralleled by the silence of the voices on stage, also engulfed by space and silence once the text has ended. Only the image of the head remains, which soon also becomes a mere shadow as the lighting fades. Beckett thereby foregrounds the threshold between the visible and the invisible, absence and presence. As in some of Beckett's subsequent drama, the performance of the narrative enacts a metamorphosis between the two. *That Time* therefore redefines and stretches to its limits the notion of dramatic action, as most of the action in the play lies in the continually shifting relationship between textual fragments and between text and stage.

The smile of the Listener at the end of the performance is unexpected and is open to a number of interpretations, once more unsettling the audience, confronting them with the uncertain and the unknown. Beckett thus destabilizes whatever codes or categories may at first be offered in order to construct a narrated universe and a position of identity within or in relation to that universe.

A PIECE OF MONOLOGUE: BEYOND THE FRAME

The variety of identities or selves in *That Time* is reduced in *A Piece of Monologue* to a series of almost identical reflections. The focus is not only on the confusion of times and identities, but on the confusion of spaces which act as the frame or ground for the appearance of the limited number of visual forms or gestures which recur throughout the play. Indeed the reproduction of identities seems to be almost entirely subordinated to the representation of a birth or origin which, having failed to bestow presence upon the Speaker, is continually repeated or reproduced in a perpetual cycle of simulations. There is a particular emphasis on the emergence, framing and perception of certain audible or visual forms against space and on their dissolution. As in *That Time*, the dynamic of difference and reproduction, whether of human life, of images or of words, is set against the increasing encroachment of darkness, stasis and death.[24]

Although the stage image in *A Piece of Monologue* features an entire human body rather than the bodily fragments of *Not I* or *That Time*, there is no movement whatsoever on stage.[25] The figure does speak, but the head is shrouded in gloom so that even the movement of the lips cannot be clearly seen. The human figure is juxtaposed with two other objects: a globe-shaped lamp, 'skull-sized white globe, faintly lit', and the pallet of a bed, only part of which is visible to the extreme right of the stage and which therefore appears to extend beyond the confines of the stage. For this reason, *A Piece of Monologue* seems to require, indeed exploit, the proscenium arch stage with its rectangular frame. The invisibility of most of the pallet foregrounds the limits of this frame and emphasizes the stage space as a framed space and the objects within it as spectacle, existing primarily to be seen. This is confirmed by the specification that all visible forms should be white, highlighting the tension between light and dark, visible form and space. Though the lamp is itself a source of light, the stage as a whole is illuminated by a 'faint diffuse light'. The faintness of the light emphasizes the effort to perceive figure and objects, while their whiteness distinguishes them, however faintly, from the darkness. The existence of these forms is therefore a function of their visibility, dependent in turn on the existence of at least some minimal degree of light.

The use of the rectangular visual frame and the objects suggesting the interior of a room recall *Ghost Trio*,[26] and indeed many of the television plays which particularly exploit the visual nature of the medium, foregrounding the camera eye, which tends to be equated with the ontologically 'hungry' eye of the subject/perceiver/creator.[27] In *Eh Joe*, Voice and camera commit a dual assault upon Joe, on the one hand forcing him to listen to the voice and on the other subjecting him, like 'O' in *Film*, to the perceiving eye of the camera, hungry for images. The image in *Ghost Trio* is more abstract, constructed from a series of rectangular visual patterns, the visual frame of the television screen echoed in the frames of door and window and in the rectangular shapes of pallet or mirror, all viewed from a variety of angles produced from a limited number of camera positions. In . . . *but the clouds* . . . the caricatural or puppet-like appearance and movements of the protagonist in his reconstructed comings and goings emphasize the nature of the image as visual construct and as object of perception. The image in these plays again draws attention to the conditions of its visibility, shifting the focus from the image itself to the unseen or implied viewer and emphasizing the duality between the object of perception and the function of perceiving or imagining.

The voice in these plays is quite distinct from the visual image of face or body. Particularly in *Ghost Trio* and in . . . *but the clouds* . . . , the voice tends to give 'stage directions' concerning the appearance of the image:

3. V: When I thought of her it was always night. I came in –
4. *Dissolve to S empty. 5 seconds. M1 in hat and greatcoat emerges from west shadow, advances five steps and stands facing east shadow. 2 seconds.*
5. V: No –
6. *Dissolve to M. 2 seconds.*
7. V: No, that is not right. When she appeared it was always night. I came in –
8. *Dissolve to S empty. 5 seconds. M1 in hat and greatcoat emerges*

from west shadow, advances five steps and stands facing east
shadow. 2 seconds.
   9. V: Right. Came in, having walked the roads since break
       of day, brought night home, stood listening. [*5*
       seconds], finally went to closet –
10. *M1 advances five steps to disappear in east shadow. 2 seconds.*[28]

The voice therefore tends to bear witness to a frequently impersonal consciousness which 'stages', indeed produces and continually reproduces the image.

Such self-conscious staging is also characteristic of *A Piece of*
Monologue: while the voice describes a figure and a setting identical
to that seen on stage, this figure is referred to in the third person
and is specifically presented as 'objectively' seen, indeed 'framed':
'Still as the lamp by his side. Gown and socks white to take faint
light. Once white. Hair white to take faint light. Foot of pallet
just visible edge of frame' (p. 267). Although the voice is not
disembodied, as it is in *That Time*, the stasis of the body on stage,
and its status as visual form, emphasize the divide between the
subject of the enunciation and the body–object. Linda Ben-Zvi
argues that *A Piece of Monologue* presents 'the schismatic self'; the
separation between the speaking subject and his 'outer' persona:

> the speaker is not the *I*, the macrocosmic figure facing the
> world and claiming the use of the first person pronoun, but
> rather the inner *me*, that objective self that watches and
> reports but has no means of independent articulation of
> being. Unlike *That Time*, where the figure at least opened
> and closed his eyes and smiled while the voices of self talked,
> and unlike *Footfalls*, where May moved as Voice spoke her
> thoughts, here there is a figure that remains impassive, like
> the figure in *Still*, while the voice within describes the man
> without.[29]

The objectification of the body is accentuated through the direct
parallel with the inanimate lamp which is of the same height and
size as the speaker and whose globe is compared to a skull in the
previously cited stage directions. While the body is reduced to a
barely visible form, the lamp assumes a certain animacy, so that
any trace of human presence is displaced from the body to the
globe and existence as a whole tends to be linked to the feeble
persistence of this light. Significantly, the only 'movement' on

stage, apart from the speaker's lips, is the gradual fading of the lamplight towards the end of the play: '*30 seconds before end of speech lamplight begins to fail*' (p. 265).

Although, as mentioned above, the description of the protagonist and the location of the narrative parallel the figure and the setting on stage, text and stage do not entirely coincide: if they did, the play would indeed lack any dramatic tension. While the stage image remains quite static, the text describes a nightly ritual, that of lighting the lamp, as well as two other scenes: the scene through the window on the night of the speaker's birth and an imagined funeral scene. Stan Gontarski argues that, in the later dramatic works, Beckett plays 'his stage characters with and especially against narrative, stage action played against speech or text'.[30] In *A Piece of Monologue*, the tension is perhaps rather between the static image framed by the stage and the images and actions which are framed in various ways within the text.

Linda Ben-Zvi points out that the text of *A Piece of Monologue* deals with present and future times, rather than with the past: 'the focus is less on a replaying of the past than on the experience of the present and the future' (p. 12). Certainly, within the text of *That Time*, the present is not directly mentioned at all, while the narrative in *A Piece of Monologue* frequently refers specifically to 'Now. This night.' Yet, as in *That Time*, the whole relationship between the temporal categories of past and present, and indeed between narrative and stage presents, becomes problematic. In *A Piece of Monologue*, the present, whether that of the stage or of the narrative, is presented as merely one frame in a series of identical frames stretching both backwards and forwards in time, between the poles of birth and death: 'Birth was the death of him. Ghastly grinning ever since. Up at the lid to come. In cradle and crib. At suck first fiasco. With the first totters. From mammy to nanny and back. All the way. Bandied back and forth. So ghastly grinning on. From funeral to funeral. To now. This night' (p. 265). 'This night' becomes almost immediately 'Every nightfall'. The 'now' of the narrative present, and indeed of the stage present, becomes engulfed in a series of identical past reflections, like a temporal equivalent of the receding image within an image. Yet the temporal distance between the moment of birth and the (however temporary) present is also emphasized, the references to funerals underlining the losses imposed by Time. The process of existence is seen not only as a continual repetition of the same, but as a series of repetitions with ever-diminishing material, a gradual process of reduction or fading: 'Dying on. No more no less. No. Less. Less to die. Ever less' (p. 98).

However, despite the evocation of vast stretches of time, the text also emphasizes the relationship or parallels between birth and death and between coming and going, where the one seems to metamorphose into the other. As in Nietzsche's theory of the eternal return, such perpetual repetition questions the very notion of beginning and close, as origin and end are continually reproduced within the cycle. This ambiguous relationship between beginning and end also characterizes the relationship between the two main scenes to which the text returns.

While the first lines of *A Piece of Monologue* are mainly concerned with the evocation of repeated cycles of movement, the first visual image presented by the text is the scene of birth, the origin of the protagonist's life in time.[31] Yet the process of birth is not itself described, but rather the room in which it implicitly occurs. Indeed, the activity of birth seems to have been displaced onto the description of the budding of the young leaves beyond the room in which presumably the protagonist has been born: 'Born dead of night. Sun long sunk behind the larches. New needles turning green. In the room dark gaining. Till faint light from standard lamp. Wick turned low' (p. 265). Death and birth, however, are also juxtaposed within the image, as Linda Ben-Zvi has noted: 'the death of the day is contrasted with the birth of the year' (p. 13).

The disappearance of the strong natural light of the sun is also contrasted with the faint light of the lamp. Again, questions of birth and death, presence and absence, are transposed from purely human terms into a register of light, the descending hierarchy from sun to gas lamp to electric lamp on stage paralleling the fading of the fullness of presence, represented by the *absent* sun which remains absent throughout the speaker's life: 'Years of nights'. Life seems, therefore, merely a shadow, a faint reflection of a barely imagined and infinitely inaccessible glorious presence: 'Sun long sunk. . . .'

The action described by the text is that of lighting the oil lamp, an action which is framed between two moments of stasis and between two darknesses. Firstly, there is the darkness which the protagonist contemplates on rising, the darkness 'outside', visually framed by the window: 'Gropes to window and stares out. Stands there staring out. Stock still staring out. Nothing stirring in that black vast' (p. 265). In the prose text *Still*, an external or imagined scene is perceived through the frame of the window, which both gives access to the scene and yet emphasizes the subject's alienation from it, locked within the room-cell: 'Sitting quite still at valley window normally turn head now and see it the sun low in the southwest sinking.'[32] In *A Piece of Monologue*, however, the scene which the protagonist contemplates beyond the window is one of unrelieved darkness. The second darkness is that into which the protagonist stares as he turns to the wall once the lamp is lit: 'Stands there staring beyond. Nothing. Empty dark' (p. 267).

The lamp-lighting sequence, supplemented by the birth and death images, constitutes the main narrative material. This material is repeated again and again within the text, but each time the pattern differs slightly.[33] The first time this ritual is described, there is no mention of blackness beyond the wall, only stasis. The wall is described as blank, though once covered with the photographs of loved ones: 'Unframed. Unglazed.' These images, however, are no more than memories, as the photographs themselves have been torn down and swept under the bed, until they are all 'gone' (the initial title of the play in English). It is significant, however, that the loved ones appear only as absent or destroyed representations: 'All gone so long. Gone. Ripped off and torn to shreds' (p. 266). Each photograph is evoked only through its absence, or rather, through the grey stain left by its trace, like the grey stain that is also left by the nightly issue of smoke from the lamp: 'Lamp smoking though wick turned low. Strange. Faint smoke issuing through vent in globe. Low ceiling stained by night after night of this' (pp. 266–7). The absence even of the image of the protagonist's parents, paralleling the absence of the light of the sun, drains his world of the security of origin and the fullness of presence, leaving merely echoes and shadows. Yet the protagonist seems not only to suffer from lack of his own or others' presence, but to reject the notion of origin or of an original birth, as the evocation of his own birth becomes increasingly indistinguishable from the nightly simulation of the process of creation through the lighting of the lamp.

This ritual is also framed by stillness and darkness. The disappearance of the photographs emphasizes the void into which the protagonist stares at the latter end of the ritual. He stares beyond the blank wall to the darkness 'beyond', bereft of all images:

65

'Stands there facing the wall staring beyond. Nothing there either. Nothing stirring there either. Nothing stirring anywhere. Nothing to be seen anywhere. Nothing to be heard anywhere' (p. 266). The sense of the perceptible world fading, the reduction of available forms, is emphasized not only by the absence of photographs, but by the lack of any perceptible forms of life. As in *Endgame*, everything seems to be running out, not just provisions, but the actual form and texture of the perceptible world.[34] Still there is as yet no end, no 'none', only lessness: 'None now. No. No such thing as none.'

The next time that the ritual is described, the actual action of lamp-lighting is glossed over and much more emphasis is placed on the static scenes, where the immobile protagonist stares into the void, both beyond the window and beyond the wall. The description of the void through the window parallels the previous description of the darkness beyond the wall. Hence the two blacknesses – that preceding and that following the lighting of the lamp – mirror each other. The distinction between text and stage is also undermined. The speaker is described in much greater detail as he stands staring at the wall: 'Still as the lamp by his side. Gown and socks white to take faint light. Once white. Hair white to take faint light. Foot of pallet just visible edge of frame. Once white to take faint light' (p. 267). This description specifically parallels the image of the speaker and the setting on stage. The mention of the visual frame echoes the borders of the stage frame, the wall beyond which the protagonist stares corresponding to the (of course illusory) 'fourth wall' of the proscenium stage.[35] The stage present therefore seems to correspond to one stage in the nightly ritual evoked by the text. The 'here and now' of the stage present becomes enveloped in the repetition of previous or subsequent stages described in the text: scenic presentation or presence is subsumed in textual representation.

The play between presentation and representation also occurs within the text. As the speaker stares into the darkness 'beyond', an image appears. This darkness therefore acts, in contrast to the framed darkness beyond the window, as the frame against which images or memories emerge, parting the darkness. Indeed, the first image to appear is that of another frame, the window: 'Then slow fade up of a faint form. Out of the dark. A window' (p. 267). This window opens onto the scene outside the room already described as that of the protagonist's birth: 'Looking west. Sun long sunk behind the larches' (p. 267). This scene therefore reappears, but with an emphasis on the frame, on its being *seen* and on its appearance/emergence from the dark. Rather than an immense distance between past and present, the past here seems to be contained, indeed created, within the (fictional) present, undermining the borders of each.

At the same time, this scene also repeats that of the protagonist staring into the 'outer' dark beyond the window described in the first part of the ritual, before the lamp-lighting sequence, although the darkness evoked there bears no trace of images. Just as the extremities of birth and death merge or metamorphose through the earlier repetition of phrases, the relationship between these two poles of the nightly ritual becomes increasingly ambiguous through the pattern of repetition. The images circle back on each other so often that it becomes impossible to talk of beginning or end, but a series of self-generating cycles, each containing those before. Yet each repetition, by modifying the pattern or by extending it, creating new levels of juxtaposition and contrast, continually changes the focus and the interpretation of what has gone before. In particular, as in *Company*, composed at the same time as *A Piece of Monologue*, what at first appears to be a contrast between 'given' and imagined forms, is progressively eroded to reveal instead different levels of fictitious construction: 'Devised deviser devising it all for company. In the same figment dark as his figments.'[36] The image of the protagonist's birth therefore becomes, on another level, the birth of the image in the process of creation/representation.

The emergence of the image is preceded by an evocation of the birth of speech: 'Till first word always the same. Night after night the same. Birth' (p. 267). This is, in fact, the first word of the text that we have been hearing. Just as the image of the birth scene reappears as framed by the window and marked as representation, so we become aware of the entire text as engaged in the process of repeating its own birth, reproducing its own beginnings. Thus, if the text tends to mask its materiality or texture as sound or verbal system through evoking visual images, the image, through these references, metamorphoses back into its literary or verbal medium. This also occurred in *That Time* where many of the repeated scenes or objects, such as the millstone, the 'pastoral' setting of the cornfield[37] or the ruin, have strong literary or semantic connotations; a process epitomized by the metamorphosis of the leaves of the wood into the leaves of the book in the Public

Library. As in *Not I*, the text emphasizes the physical sensation, even sensuality of voice or speech production, the laboured birth of the word: '. . . waiting for first word. It gathers in his mouth. Parts lips and thrusts tongue between them. Tip of tongue. Feel soft touch of tongue on lips. Of lips on tongue' (p. 268). It is as if the whole process of impregnation and expulsion were simultaneously reproduced in the birth of the word.

Just as in the first evocation of the scene outside the window at birth, the actual birth was displaced on to the image of the budding leaves, in the later sequence where there is no mention of leaves, it is displaced on to the ritual of lighting the lamp, which now becomes a symbol of birth/creation: 'There in the end slowly a faint hand. Holding aloft a lighted spill. In the light of spill faintly the hand and milk white globe' (p. 267). The use of the word 'spill' suggests that the lamp is being lit by other hands (the father's?) on the evening of the protagonist's birth. In this repetition of the ritual, only the hands are seen. Because of the lack of specificity, the scene is associated not only with birth, but with the original Genesis, as the mysterious hand lights the globe and subsequently withdraws, abandoning its creation: 'Pale globe alone in gloom.'

The image fades and darkness is restored, but only temporarily. The dark parts once more to reveal a contrasting scene; that of a funeral, mentioned earlier and now described in greater detail: 'Till dark slowly parts again. Grey light. Rain pelting. Umbrellas round a grave. Seen from above. Streaming black canopies. Black ditch beneath' (p. 268). This is the only scene in daylight and it picks up the image of the rain, previously associated with mercy, through the reference to Portia's famous speech from *The Merchant of Venice*: 'Rain some nights still slant against the panes. Or dropping gentle on the place beneath' (p. 266). As with the birth image, the visual perspective and the implied 'directions' within the text announce these images as simulated or constructed. A later repetition of this image specifies: 'Coffin out of frame.' The lack of verbs also transforms the action into a series of image 'stills'. Like the birth scene, the image fades and dark is restored. These framed images of birth and death are contrasted with the unblemished dark, as the lamp-lighting scene is also prescribed by darkness.

As Linda Ben-Zvi notes, throughout the text the references to birth become briefer and the image of the funeral becomes more detailed: 'Just as the first mention of birth in the play is the most detailed (with each becoming progressively more vague until the word remains unuttered), such is Beckett's attention to balance in the work that the first mention of funerals is general, whilst each subsequent reference becomes more detailed until it virtually subsumes the images of birth' (p. 15). However, the repetition not only privileges the funeral scene, but also places an increasing emphasis on moments of stasis, in particular, the immobility of the protagonist lost in contemplation of the darkness and its images, associated with the latter stages of the ritual. Yet beginning and end again intersect as the different stages of the ritual become confused, through the pattern of the repetition, as the two darknesses, that preceding the lamp-lighting sequence and that following it, begin to merge. Moreover, the same confusion affects the lamp-lighting sequence itself, which now combines phrases formerly used to summarize the protagonist's actions with those used of the mysterious creator: 'Spill. Hands. Lamp. Gleam of brass. Pale globe alone in gloom' (p. 269). Beckett seems to be parodying the Cartesian cogito which posits itself as its own origin: 'The cogito is the originary act of legitimation of the subject, who simply takes the place of origin: a beginning without a trace of what went before, and therefore capable of reproducing itself in an always present perpetuity.'[38] The Speaker, however, is displaced from the centre of his own discourse – creating only diminishing fragments of a figure and a visual context. Even these are gradually erased as the visual elements of the stage and narrated image become engulfed by darkness. Representation here fades into a ghostly ritual, attempting to capture the last echoes of a trace of presence before making a final exit.

The repetition of the funeral scene implies, as Ben-Zvi suggests, a future, a movement or, as in *That Time*, a departure: 'Where soon to be. This night to be' (p. 269). This imagined departure is paralleled ironically by the increasing emphasis on the stasis of the protagonist: 'stands there stock still staring out as if unable to move again' (p. 268). Each time the scene is repeated, death is a little nearer, emphasized by the references to the 'last' appearance of the images, 'As if looking his last' (p. 268), and by the announced approach of the coffin, as yet 'out of frame', as if the protagonist is now staging his own burial.

The desire to be gone is also associated with the darkness finally emptied of all images, of all objects of perception. The text suggests that this darkness is to be reached through a renting in turn of the boundary, frame or veil between life and death, between the space divided and continually animated by the cycles of repetition and representation and the 'further dark' of death, which seems to promise an end to the exile of the subject in the margins and mazes of identity and fiction. 'There staring at that black veil. Waiting on the rip word.' Ben-Zvi refers to the 'pun on RIP, *requiescat in pace*, which suggests that death is the final way of ripping the dark, of piercing that "outer blackness". The outer darkness, Beckett seems to indicate, may be "ripped" by death, but as long as man lives, he can only temporarily part the dark' (p. 15). The text emphasizes, however, that this renting is to be produced by the text: the speaker waits, not on the word of birth, but on the word which will release him from all reincarnations and all reproductions – the 'rip word'.

In 'The Rip Word in *A Piece of Monologue*',[39] Kristin Morrison interprets the 'rip word' in relation to 'rip tide' and sees it as 'that disturbance in the flow of language which reveals what is hidden, the unpleasant or discreditable truth which may be disguised or submerged but never completely evaded' (p. 349). She therefore argues that the rip word is the word 'Begone', the word which reveals the truth the speaker had been avoiding: 'the imminence of his own death' (p. 354). Indeed, if, on the contrary, the speaker's death is openly desired, the 'rip word' may draw on the literal meaning of rip as 'to tear', supplemented by the connotations of other rent veils throughout literature or history: the 'veil of Maya', or the temple veil rent on the death of Christ.

The final phrases of the text emphasize the lack of presence throughout the speaker's life, his entire existence is seen as composed of shadows: 'Ghost Light. Ghost nights. Ghost rooms. Ghost graves. He almost said . . . ghost loved ones' (p. 269). As in *That Time*, the stretches of time at first evoked, the thirty thousand nights and two and a half billion seconds, become as nothing, as brief and ambiguous as the audience's experience of the performance, nearing an end as the light begins to die on stage. Both plays testify to the sense of a creative tradition founded on presence and origin which has almost burned itself out, leaving only a last few flickers of light amidst the ashes. Perhaps significantly, after each of these plays, Beckett's return to drama featured a female voice or voices. Discussing the feminization of contemporary (masculine) philosophical discourse, Rosi Braidotti notes that 'the modern subject, the split subject, discovers the feminine layer of his own thought just as he loses the mastery he used to assume as his own'.[40]

3

THIS SEX WHICH IS NOT ONE

Within a language pervasively masculinist, a phallogocentric language, women represent the *unrepresentable*. In other words, women represent the sex that cannot be thought, a linguistic absence and opacity.[1]

Now the/a woman who does not have *one* sex [*sexe*] – which will usually have been interpreted as meaning no sex – cannot subsume it/herself under *one* term, generic or specific. Body, breasts, pubis, clitoris, labia, vulva, vagina, neck of the uterus, womb . . . and this nothing which already makes them take pleasure in/from their apartness [jouir dans/de leur écart] thwarts their reduction to any proper name, any specific meaning, any concept.[2]

The plays explored in the previous chapters seem to be haunted by the ghost of the paternal *logos*, which animates the drive towards self-hood, knowledge and truth. However, while some of Beckett's plays foreground the petrification of logocentric structures of authority and identity, others focus more on the underside of power and authority, the neglected spaces and margins of representation. Within Western patriarchal history, the repressed feminine is inextricably linked to the very concept of other spaces. Rosi Braidotti notes that 'at times of crisis every culture tends to turn to its "others", to become feminized, in the sense of having to face its limitations, gaps and deficiencies'.[3] In this sense, Beckett can be seen as having adopted a 'feminized' practice. Central to this issue is the question of the relationship between the Symbolic and the Other. Is this a stable, unchangeable opposition, or is it subject to negotiation and change?

As some feminist critics of psychoanalysis have noted, psychoanalysis has tended to rely on certain laws which are taken as 'given', such as the Oedipus complex. This tends to reinforce the establishment of the patriarchal Symbolic as the only route to signification, whatever the cost in repression. It also grounds the Symbolic in irreparable loss. Judith Butler suggests that the Lacanian model is one of religious tragedy, where the subject is condemned to obedience by the ómniscient Law, but where the tasks set by the Law, such as the assumption of coherent identity, are impossible to achieve:

> The Symbolic [is] that which operates for human subjects as the inaccessible but all-determining deity. . . . This structure of religious tragedy in Lacanian theory effectively undermines any strategy of cultural politics to configure an alternative imaginary for the play of desires. . . . There is, of course, a comic side to this drama that is revealed through the disclosure of the permanent impossibility of the realisation of identity. But even this comedy is the inverse expression of an enslavement to a God that it claims to be unable to overcome.[4]

Beckett's presentation of the relation between the Symbolic and the Other has similarities with this tragic-parodic model. His concern with fragmentation, loss and *manque-à-être* suggests an irreparable lack of being which is always at odds with the structures of representation. These structures seem to be ordained by omnipotent patriarchal figures who condemn their creatures to impossible attempts to 'realize identity'. The figures of power and authority in Beckett's plays are almost exclusively male – Godot, Pozzo, Hamm, the Director. Some figures of authority cannot be placed within recognizable gender frames – the Light in *Play*, for example, or the representation of the voice of Bam in *What Where*. However, in both of these cases, the signifier, Light or microphone, refers primarily to a creative or juridical function which follows a logocentric model even in order to parody it. As numerous feminist writers insist, issues of power and gender cannot be separated, since the Symbolic order is constructed on the repression of the feminine as maternal body and as the Other which must be excluded for the identity and the voice of the One to be asserted, resulting in an imbalance between the male and the female gender in their historical relation to authority and representation: 'The rejection, the exclusion of a female imaginary certainly puts woman in the position of experiencing herself only fragmentarily, in the little-structured margins of a dominant ideology, as waste, or excess, what is left of a mirror invested by the (masculine) "subject" to reflect himself, to copy himself.'[5]

Braidotti argues that contemporary philosophy has turned to the feminine in order to renew itself through gaining access to new discursive fields: 'the feminine is thus posited as a sign opening up unexplored territories.'[6] Several articles in the recent study of *Women in Beckett*[7] analyse the shift in Beckett's work from his rather stereotypical portrayal of women characters in the early fiction as lustful flesh-bound predators luring the male narrator from his creative or spiritual quest, to his frequent portrayal of women as central characters in the drama after *Happy Days*.[8] However impoverished and itinerant the narrators of the early fiction may be, they claim, even in order to parody, an immense and exclusively male textual heritage. Perhaps, in the same way that Beckett shifted from the English to the French language in order to dispossess himself of his English textual heritage, he adopted the historically excluded female position in his drama in order to explore the alienation of the female subject in relation to self, language and representation.

While such a practice rejects the mastery associated with the Symbolic and privileges the feminine as a site of resistance, it may also confirm the feminine as that which is always subject to the dominant law. In this sense, the universalization of that which opposes patriarchy as 'the feminine' or even 'the Other' may be counterproductive, refusing the possibility of a changing relationship between dominant and dissident positions. Beckett can therefore be aligned more with the criticism and parody of European post-Enlightenment epistemology than with the liberation and empowerment of those marginalized by that epistemology. However, while Beckett remains epistemologically trapped in a kind of shadow dance with the Other, his dramatic practice, poised between tragedy, parody and poetry, continually questions the rules by which dominant forms of representation are constructed and forges new languages through which the repressed or excluded may be articulated. The two plays explored in this chapter focus on Beckett's exploration of the 'feminine' position in relation to identity and language. In *Come and Go* the three female characters have no individual identity – they are little more than three shades and their voices little more than echoes of each other. In *Not I*,

by contrast, this lack of identity does not fade into shades of
absence but is the animating force for a radical disruption of the
stable visual and verbal categories of the Symbolic.

NOT I: STAGING THE FEMININE – FROM EXCESS TO ABSENCE

Not I is the dramatic text most frequently discussed in the context
of Beckett's representation of female characters. Critics range
between an interpretation of the play as a sympathetic portrayal
of marginality and dispossession to a voyeuristic exploitation of
the feminine as lack.[9] It seems to me that the fascination of *Not I*
lies in its articulation both of the intense inner experience of a
particular subject and of a complex network of associations and
issues relating to gender and the representation of women and the
'feminine' within Western culture.

In *Not I,* the body is reduced to the fragmented image of a
mouth suspended in darkness and the rhythm of the text uttered
by Mouth becomes increasingly frantic, exceeding linguistic structures of control. Yet Mouth is suspended in the space of the stage,
watched by the shadowy figure of the Auditor and, as in a trial,
apparently required to give an account of herself and her life.
There is therefore an opposition between this framework of authority and Mouth's failure or refusal to conform which engages
many of the issues outlined above.

The visual image of the mouth in *Not I*, alienated and displaced
from the 'whole' of the body, is the very opposite of the stable,
specular imago with which, according to Lacanian theory, the ego
wishes to identify. As Paul Lawley has noted, the Mouth has no
form as such: 'in itself it is a no-thing, a "no matter", an absence.'[10]
Surrounded by space and suspended in the darkness, thereby disorienting any attempt on the spectator's part to identify it with
an unseen body, it forms an image of lack or incompleteness, as
the two lips constitute a split or gap. According to Lacan, desire
or the essential division or lack in the subject, may appear within
the Imaginary, both as Melanie Klein's 'part-objects' and as
'object(s) *a*': images which contain or reveal absence and incompleteness. Lacan's 'object(s) *a*' have no fixed specular form and
are:

the result of a cut (coupure) expressed in the anatomical

mark (trait) of a margin or border – lips, 'the enclosure of the teeth', the rim of the anus, the tip of the penis, the vagina, the slit formed by the eye-lids, even the horn-shaped aperture of the ear. . . . Observe that this mark of the cut is no less obviously present in the object described by analytic theory: the mamilla, faeces, the phallus (imaginary object), the urinary flow. (An unthinkable list, if one adds, as I do, the phoneme, the gaze, the voice – the nothing.) . . . These objects have one common feature in my elaboration of them – they have no specular image, or, in other words, alterity. It is what enables them to be the 'stuff', or rather the lining, though not in any sense the reverse, of the very subject that one takes to be the subject of consciousness. For this subject, who thinks he can accede to himself by designating himself in the statement, is no more than such an object.[11]

While *Not I* operates on the level of a particular gendered figure – the old woman whose experiences are narrated, however fragmentarily, in the text, emphasizing her exclusion from certain social and juridical institutions (the supermarket or the courtroom) – on a more theoretical level, the abstract, non-naturalistic representation of Mouth shifts the focus onto questions of gender and representation. If Mouth can be interpreted as a voyeuristic castration of the female,[12] [she] may also be interpreted as an attempt to present the confusion of the subject confronted with [her] alienation from particular signifying positions within language and gender. While both 'she' and Mouth seem to be presented in negative terms, Beckett's exposure and questioning of the ways our inherited linguistic and visual apparatus constructs a value-laden conceptual universe, challenges that negativity.

Returning to a more Kristevan perspective, Mouth can be seen not only as 'lack', but as a disruptive force which threatens the conceptual stability and fixity established by the Symbolic. Psychoanalysis suggests that the distinction between inside and outside, container and contained, is essential to the construction of both the Imaginary and the Symbolic orders.[13] However, in *Not I* these conceptual categories break down, as Mouth evokes simultaneously a number of bodily orifices, on the threshold between inner and outer. There is an emphasis on the flow (whether of speech or other emissions) from inside to outside, destabilizing the categories of container and contained, or indeed the categories of inside and outside, emphasizing the failure to control or contain this flow.

Luce Irigaray has stressed the opposition between the fluid and that which has solid, unified form: 'Thus fluid is always in a relation of excess or lack *vis-à-vis* unity.'[14] She also emphasizes that philosophic discourse has tended to repress the fluid and to privilege rational conceptual structures which are founded on a phallocentric imaginary of the solid, the 'one' and the 'same': 'what structuration of (the) language does not maintain a *complicity of long standing between rationality and a mechanics of solids alone?* [p. 107]. . . . Fluid – like that other, inside/outside of philosophical discourse – is, by nature, unstable' (p. 112). Irigaray therefore links the fluid with the feminine and with the vagina in particular: '*Since that which is in excess with respect to form – for example, the feminine sex – is necessarily rejected as beneath or beyond the system currently in force*' (pp. 110–11).

The disturbing impact of the image of Mouth can be linked both to the uncontrollable flow of its utterances and to its open, 'gaping' nature. Luce Irigaray has written of the tendency (particularly of male writers) to use the image of the vagina to represent the horror of both excess and absence. On the one hand, woman is inscribed in representation as 'waste or excess'. On the other, due to the privileging of phallocentric specularization, the female 'sex' also represents '*the horror of nothing to see*'.[15] Beckett both uses or exploits this negative iconography in the image of Mouth – her position on stage apparently offers her as a negative spectacle, and yet he defuses the power relations inherent within it by reversing the repression of lack or excess, which becomes the major dynamic principle of the play. While apparently being judged by the Symbolic as lacking or excessive to its rules, Mouth may also be judging the Symbolic, refusing the language it offers her to speak herself in.

While the stage image presents a visual representation of the lacking and fragmented subject, the text presents the subject's attempts to tell a life-story Mouth repeatedly denies as her own. As in *Play*, the text of *Not I* juxtaposes the narration of scenes from the past, with reflection on the present act of narration. There is a strong visual contrast between the descriptions of the past and the darkness in which 'she' found herself following the extinction of the light in the April meadow. These sections of the narration correspond closely to what the audience sees before them. These contrasting scenes are not divided into separate sections, as in *Play*, but rather scenes from the past referred to by Beckett as 'life-scenes'[16] are juxtaposed with the narration of the subject's experience in the darkness throughout the five 'movements' of the text. These are demarcated by Mouth's repeated denials of the story she narrates and the Auditor's subsequent four gestures of helplessly raising his arms. Paul Lawley has argued that the experience of the play lies precisely in the 'counterpoint between two dramatic dimensions: that of the text, in which we are told the story of She, and that of the stage image',[17] a counterpoint also within the text between the visual and the verbal, between past and present, between silence and speech and between absence and the flux of visual/verbal forms.

The first section of *Not I* is mainly narrative, with several references to chronology: 'before her time', 'eight months later', 'coming up to sixty when – ... what? seventy?' (p. 216). However, the narrative revolves around absence: 'godforsaken hole called ... no matter', 'parents unknown', 'no love of any kind'. The old woman herself is presented as absence within: 'stare into space', 'stand there waiting', 'mouth half open as usual'. Within the life-scenes, whether in the meadow, the supermarket or the courtroom, the divorce or distance between the subject and her body is stressed. Paul Lawley has noted both the objectification of the body and the frequent references to the fragmented body within the text:

> The adjustment 'the *bag* back in her hand' directs attention to a strange effect: 'mouth half open as usual ... till it was back in her hand' gives us a momentary surrealistic image, as does the earlier 'just hand in the list', where the verb 'hand' feels briefly like a noun. It is as though She is shopping for the missing parts of Mouth's body.... Throughout the play, the fragmentary discourse throws up a fragmented body, the image of a fragmented self.[18]

This fragmentation is also characteristic of the old woman's view of the external world. In the supermarket scene, for example, there is no overall or totalized image of the external scene. The point of view varies from a general view of the shoppers 'busy shopping centre ... supermart ...' to a 'close-up' of individual objects such as the shopping list or the 'old black shopping bag'. The images are given no precise spatio-temporal position and the lack of 'wholeness' is emphasized by the broken, incomplete syntax

of the entire text. These scenes therefore emphasize the lack of a
centre of specularization or of desire. If the fragmented objects
within these scenes betray the psychic investment characteristic of
the pre-verbal Imaginary, where the self is not yet differentiated
from the external world, they seem to lack any positionality (however decentred) of desire. The subject is presented as entirely
passive, as pure lack, rather than as lacking. The absence of desire
is linked to the absence of perception and speech.

However, the two accounts of the meadow scene, towards the
end of the old woman's life, focus on moments of intense visual
perception on the part of the old woman, the first of which significantly occurs just before the narration of the advent of words in
the 'underworld' in which Mouth finds herself. In this scene, the
old woman stares at a distant spire, her bodily motion contrasted
with her attempt to visually fix the object of her gaze, at the
moment when she seems to become aware that it is slipping away
from her: 'that April morning . . . she fixing with her eye . . . a
distant bell . . . as she hastened towards it . . . fixing it with her
eye . . . lest it elude her . . .' (p. 218). The consciousness of visual
perception seems to anticipate the eruption of the processes of
speech. Paul Lawley has pointed out the similarity between the
motion of the eyelids (no eye) to that of the two lips we see before
us: 'the mechanics of the eye find their visual referent in the mouth
we are looking at.'[19] Indeed, in the final 'life-scene', in the public
conveniences, the old woman's silence and inner absence become
a 'steady stream . . . mad stuff . . . half the vowels wrong . . .'
(p. 222). The vacancy of the Eye/I has therefore become the
uncontrollable outpouring of the Mouth.

This transformation within the 'life-scenes' is repeated within
the narrative of the darkness, which traces the same progression
as that of the light: from the silent eye to the advent of words.
Elizabeth Wright, in her book *Psychoanalytic Criticism*, cites the play
as a representation of the inescapable repetition of the primary
splitting of the subject, on its entry into visual and linguistic
symbolization:

Mouth is reliving the trauma of the primordial moment when
the body senses its split from the Real. This experience can
neither be included in the Imaginary, the realm of illusory
wholeness, nor can it be part of the Symbolic, the domain
which grants a conditional identity. The traumatic moment

79

can thus return in psychosis as the experience of the 'fragmented body', unique for every subject, remainder and
reminder of this fracture, appearing in art as images of gro-
tesque dismemberment . . . . Language both reveals and con-
ceals the fracture. For Lacan, narrative is the attempt to
catch up retrospectively on this traumatic separation, to tell
this happening again and again, to re-count it: the narrative
of the subject caught in the net of signifiers. . . .[20]

The narrative as a whole pivots around and continually returns
to the moment or process of birth, simultaneously that of the infant
'tiny little thing', repeated several times as the narrative returns
to its beginning, and that of speech, which is twice recounted
within the narrative – the old woman's outpouring in the public
lavatories and Mouth's invasion by words – but which is also
continually *reproduced* on stage in the flood of words from the spotlit
mouth. The chronology of the narrative is therefore disrupted, as
the categories and divisions of past and present, light and dark,
narrative and stage image dissolve into the steady stream of words
being produced in the here and now of the performance, preventing
any attempt to create order or coherence, whether by Mouth's
brain, the Auditor or the audience. This disruption is emphasized
by the rejection of punctuation and the laws of syntax in the text,
where each phrase is elided, never achieving completion or closure.
    The passive female subject of the narrative and the negative
spectacle of Mouth in *Not I* are therefore transformed into and
through a process of *production* – of text, meaning and utterance
itself.[21] This production is both represented in the text and constituted by the text, which seems to generate the organs necessary
to produce speech: 'gradually she felt . . . her lips moving . . .
imagine! . . her lips moving! . . as of course till then she had not . . .
and not alone the lips . . . the cheeks . . . the jaws . . . the whole
face . . . all those contortions without which . . . no speech possible'
(p. 219). Indeed the world, the body and the narrative are not
simply transformed into text, but created or produced by the text.
Mouth's performance destabilizes the representative and perceptual conventions of spectacle and narrative which historically work
towards the exclusion, devalorization and indeed punishment of
areas of experience and behaviour not authorized by those conventions.
    This destabilization of conceptual and perceptual categories

reinforces the presentation of the voice/body/text as fluid excretion. Within the text, the stream of words is specifically compared to the disposal of waste in a public lavatory. As Keir Elam suggests, Beckett thereby devalues the dignity and authority of the logos, the word/law of the Father, world and word transformed into excrement or waste: 'Her earlier anal-verbal retentiveness ("she who but a moment before . . . but a moment! . . . could not make a sound") gives way violently and publicly to a kind of dia-loghorrhea ("can't stop").'[22]

At the same time, the shadow of paternal authority continues to haunt *Not I*. Julia Kristeva balances the disintegration of the logos with the continued desire for meaning which maintains the dynamic. She argues in 'The Father, Love and Banishment'[23] that Mouth is haunted by the absent father/Father, whose Death is the foundation of all meaning (as the phallus only permits signification through its absence), but from which she is exiled. She is therefore doomed to 'the pursuit of a paternal shadow binding her to the body and language' (p. 154), even though body and language, deprived of centre or meaning, are transformed into uncontrolled excrement or waste. Mouth's anxiety, and indeed that of the audience, is related to her inability to escape or reject the shadow of paternal authority which maintains the eye of judgement and legislates on what is significant and what is meaningless, who is to be saved and who cast out.

There is a corresponding ambiguity throughout the play between the gaze of judgement and the subversion or deflection of that gaze. The confrontation between the subject observed and the observing look characterizes the life-scenes narrated in the text. In the scenes in the supermarket and in the courtroom the old woman is observed and judged, 'stand up woman . . . speak up woman . . .', but returns no gaze of her own – her eyes are empty, 'staring into space'. In the scene in the lavatory, however, the empty look has become a flood of speech which she directs at her auditors – 'till she saw the stare she was getting . . . then die of shame . . . crawl back in . . .'. Likewise, in the narrative of Mouth's experiences 'in the dark', at first her eyelids open and close, but there is no gaze. Shortly afterwards, however, the word-flood which constitutes her performance on stage begins. The two lips continually opening and closing recall the description of the eyelids in the text and, indeed, Mouth seems almost to be staring at the audience. However, the gaze of judgement which positions subject and is transformed into an excessive flow of speech which eschews the central, controlling position of the 'I'.

This foregrounding of the process of looking draws attention to the act of spectatorship within the theatre. The frantic mouth is contrasted with the completely calm and immobile image of the Auditor, a silent figure dressed in a long black djellaba, positioned diagonally across the stage space from the mouth. The relationship between Auditor and Mouth is ambiguous and some have seen [him][24] as part of Mouth's drama, identified as the interlocutor of her narrative. However, although [he] gestures four times to Mouth, there seems to be little evidence of any direct intervention. The Auditor is defined primarily by his function – that of listener. This again tends to present Mouth as producer of speech rather than purely as spectacle. Although the Auditor forms part of the visual image of the play, the fact that [he] is dimly lit and [his] figure cloaked discourages the audience from focusing on the Auditor as spectacle. Rather, [he] contributes to the conceptual ambiguities that the play effects. [His] gender is uncertain, [his] relation to Mouth is uncertain and he draws attention to the ambiguous role of the audience, since [he] reflects the audience's role back at them from within the performance. Like the audience, [he] exists to perceive and interpret Mouth's performance, although [he] is also part of the performance that the audience is trying to perceive and interpret. While the audience in more traditional drama remains in a privileged position outside the dramatic world offered for their entertainment or judgement, Beckett continually emphasizes the implication of the audience in the process of constructing or failing to construct and interpret that world. The audience may appear to be privileged and detached observers of Mouth's disorder, but Beckett both frames and subverts that role.

If the Auditor reflects the audience's listening function, in the narrated lavatory scene the audience's gaze is reflected back at them in the image of Mouth's spectators as 'an assembly of gapers in a place of public convenience'.[25] Like the skull in Holbein's painting, used by Lacan to illustrate his notion of 'the look',[26] the audience is also being looked at, their complacency and apparent autonomy as the all seeing eye are challenged. Beckett further undermines the authority of the audience as they, like the ear and the brain in the text, are unable to hear or understand a large part of Mouth's speech. They are themselves mirrored or multiplied in and reduced to the separate *functions* of Auditor and the fragmented organs evoked in and by the text: the ear straining to hear, the eye fixed on the mouth and the brain trying to piece it all together. Yet, unless they leave the theatre, they are unable to escape their role as spectator. Like Mouth, they are held in position by the framework of theatre and the role it casts for them, yet Beckett ensures that the audience are as incapable of fulfilling that role as Mouth is of fulfilling hers. Both are condemned for the duration of the play to the impossible struggle to make sense and order out of Mouth's chaotic stream of speech.

Not I therefore maintains a tension between what Josette Féral describes as 'specific symbolic structures'[27] and the disruptive dynamic of performance: 'Performance can be seen as an art form whose primary aim is to undo "competencies" (which are primarily theatrical). Performance readjusts these competencies and redistributes them in a desystematized arrangement.'[28] Chantal Pontbriand describes performance as a process of 'disarticulation or dismemberment'.[29] Beckett is thereby also redefining theatrical presence. Mouth's presence is not that of a 'literal, coherent, centralised character'[30]. Yet we are acutely aware of the perceptual realities, however minimal, of light, image and voice, which disrupt the signifying economy of the Symbolic. Helga Finter analyses the way in which a 'semioticization of the inexpressible' in the theatre forces the audience to reposition itself in relation to the text – to become aware of the material qualities of the text as voice:

> listening to the voice-sound can mean the loss of listening to the voice-speech, comprehension of meaning; and listening to the voice-speech can occur at the expense of understanding sound. In the same manner, the attention one gives to the voice diminishes the attention one gives to the visual. After this splitting up, which recalls an anterior stage of the subject, the perception of the sound-image-speech will have to be reorganised for each of the auditors/spectators.[31]

By foregrounding the materiality of the voice and the processes of utterance, rather than the symbolic 'object' of the text as object of desire, the audience is forced to confront voice, self and reality as constructed and produced through language. While apparently offered as negative spectacle, Mouth's performance disrupts the apparatus of perception and judgement which would enable the audience to exercise any position of authority, as she fails or refuses to adopt such a position herself.

COME AND GO: A PATTERN OF SHADES

The rhythm of *Come and Go* is quite different to that of *Not I*. While Mouth in *Not I* produces an excess of speech, in *Come and Go* there are hardly any words at all. While written before *Not I*, *Come and Go*, more than the later play, anticipates Beckett's ghost plays of the 1970s and 1980s, which are concerned with the borders between the visible and the invisible, presence and absence, sound and silence. The text of *Come and Go*, which is the most minimal of any of the plays studied here,[32] seems to exist only to emphasize the unspoken, the insubstantiality of the three figures' existences, to which no words can give even the appearance of substance. The play as a whole evokes depths of silence and absence through the continual gaps and spaces opened up by its minimal patterns of speech and movement and through its use of zones of light and darkness. The perceptual indeterminacy created on stage in these plays therefore becomes as important as the shifting of identities and the undermining of conceptual categories within the text. Indeed, the uncertainty of presence which characterizes this and many of Beckett's subsequent plays is presented as much through the texture of the performance – through patterns of lighting or movement – as through the text.

The original drafts of *Come and Go*, however, reveal a very different tone and texture. The stage directions, whereby each figure exits in turn leaving the other two together, are already mapped out in one of the first two drafts,[33] but both are characterized by a quite different tone from the published play. Rosemary Pountney refers to their 'hilarious revue-like style'.[34] The two women remaining on stage exchange sexual confidences, as well as commiserations about the fate of the third, in a tone summarized by the above critic: 'all three women should both gossip and be gossiped about.'[35] The dialogue consists for the most part of empty clichés reminiscent of *Play*, written between two and three years earlier. A recurrent refrain of both drafts is: 'Very much so. [*complacent laugh.*] Very much so indeed.' The illicit loves mentioned by each of the three women, a discharged prisoner, a croquet champion and possibly, Rosemary Pountney suggests, a visit to a brothel – 'Well! Is that place going still?' – are contrasted with the husbands phoning in distress from Madeira or Naples or encountered at the Gaiety. The adultery theme of *Play* therefore recurs in these early versions. The sexual motif and distinctly mannered, parodic tone are emphasized in one of these drafts by the inclusion of readings from a novel in the 'romantic-erotic'[36] style.

However, during the writing or rewriting process, which included at least fifteen versions, the text was gradually stripped of almost all of its circumstantial detail. The final text contains little more than 120 words in all. As Hersch Zeifman comments: 'Beckett has pared the play of all superfluities, has shed layer after excess layer until what remains is only the barest minimum of dramatic form.'[37] The women are transformed from complacent gossips and adulteresses to fragile, contemplative aged or ageless maidens who only dream of love. This transformation seems to parallel the shift from such garrulous female characters as Maddy Rooney or Winnie, flesh-bound despite their desire for dissolution or flight, in Beckett's earlier plays to the ghost maidens of *Footfalls* or *Rockaby* – although a May-like character associated with Schubert's 'Death and the Maiden' ('All alone in that ruinous old house') is mentioned in *All That Fall*. Instead of identifying female characters with materiality and predatory sexuality Beckett seems to have become interested in the female position in relation to representation as one of lack and exclusion. It is following this shift that women become subjects in Beckett's drama. This parallels the development of Beckett's presentation of the body, which is largely a restrictive material encumbrance in the early work, alligned (with women) as object in contrast to the (masculine) speaking subject. However, in the later plays, the body becomes the site and sign of subjectivity, both subject and object, on the borderline between the material and the imaginative, between desire and representation.

Starting off from material which is reminiscent of the narrative of *Play*, *Come and Go* becomes a minimal but highly allusive text which emphasizes pattern and texture – the interrelation of silence and speech, light and dark, movement and stillness. The musical quality of the play is increased by visual and textual symmetry, yet at the same time, through the very strictness and regularity of the pattern, an almost mathematical framework is established which seems not only to displace the emotional content of the work from character to rhythm or pattern, but also to counteract the seduction of the lyrical quality of the text and perhaps to guard against any traces of sentimentality. Many of the later plays likewise combine a highly poetic text with a strictly regular rhythmic patterning of text, scenic movement and lighting. Fade-ups and fade-outs are timed to the second. The technical processes of production play with and against the presentation of subjectivity – subjectivity is therefore placed within a performance system which reframes traditional categories of 'character'.[38] Paul Newham contrasts 'naturalism's mono-centric obsession with the presentation of a single character' with the performance style of contemporary non-traditional theatre in which, as in *Come and Go*, 'the notion of character [becomes] less important than other dimensions such as kinetics, light and shape – dimensions which [have] always been the substance of sculpture and painting, but which within performance had hitherto been central only to dance'.[39]

Come and Go largely eludes the conventions of narrative and identity, although the play draws on rather traditional associations of fragile, unfulfilled elderly maidens. We learn very little about the three women sitting side by side on stage, except that they shared a past at their girlhood school, Miss Wade's, and a particular ritual of holding hands. Whatever words remain serve simply to evoke a past or present life which is or has been so nebulous that it escapes words altogether:

VI: When did we three last meet?
RU: Let us not speak.

(p. 194)

The absence of words emphasizes the lack of a centre of individual subjectivity on the part of the three women and tends to confirm their alienation from the dominant structures of language. In previous plays, the characters have attempted to create a past for themselves, and therefore a temporally coherent identity through narrative. In *Come and Go*, the text evokes the past of the three women only to erase it: here there is no variety of past times, whether remembered or imagined. Their past has no features, in it nothing can be seen or remembered except for the most shadowy details:

FLO: Just sit together as we used to, in the playground at Miss Wade's.
RU: On the log.

(p. 194)

Indeed, the sole image which emerges from the past, that of the

86

three girls sitting side by side, finds its reflection in the stage image. The stage directions specify that the women should be seated side by side on a kind of bench, but 'as little visible as possible. It should not be clear what they are sitting on' (p. 196). Once the log is mentioned in the text, the parallels between past and present begin to emerge, confirmed by the linking of arms at the end of the play. The present seems simply an echo of the former epoque, itself composed of dreams:

RU: Holding hands . . . That way.
FLO: Dreaming . . . of love.
Silence.

(p. 195)

Before the play ends, however, Flo comments 'I can feel the rings', while the stage directions specify that the hands should be specially made up to emphasize that no rings are visible. This contradiction emphasizes both the figures' absorption in a dream world (where they do wear rings) and the absence and lack of definition of their actual existence.

The shared dreams of past and present evoked during the moments when all three women are on stage together are contrasted with the revelation that all are doomed shortly to die, the fate of each one being discussed by the other two while she briefly leaves the stage. As Rosemary Pountney comments, the imminence of their death confirms the incompleteness of their life: 'Precisely the tragedy of the women in *Come and Go* is that they appear perpetually to have been waiting for an event, possibly marriage, that never happened. And now, with death looming an unwanted lover in the shade they seem to be about to die before having ever fully lived.'[40]

In previous versions, specific reference was made to a terminal disease: 'Three months (*Pause*) at the outside.'[41] In the final version, however, nothing is stated, only intimations of mortality:

FLO: What do you think of Vi?
RU: I see little change. [*Flo moves to centre seat, whispers in
      Ru's ear. Appalled.*] Oh! Does she not realize?
FLO: God grant not.

(p. 194)

James Knowlson notes: 'The unspoken nature of the condemnation in the final version is the more powerful precisely because it is less

87

explicit.'[42] The stage directions emphasize that the exclamations on hearing the other's fate, and subsequent enquiry as to whether or not she knows, are the sole expressions of emotion or indeed variation of tone in a predominantly monotone and barely audible delivery. Yet even this brief eruption of emotion or shock at the approach of Death is quickly suppressed. The gesture of raising the finger to the lips reimposes silence. However, the fact that the figures repress their shock at the other's fate, which they do not realize is also their own, and which is implied rather than stated, tends to displace its expression onto the audience, who are left to imagine the unspoken. The text therefore serves to evoke layers of implication and of absence, as the overwhelming sense of lack – of love or of life – repressed by the speakers floods back nevertheless during the silences.

Despite the sparseness of the dialogue, Beckett has woven many literary references into the text, which haunt the play like so many verbal shades. The dominance of flower imagery evokes traditional associations of fading and fragility: the 'Good Heavens' manuscript contains reference to a Mrs Flower, while the three figures are simply designated A, B and C. The (presumably) subsequent version[43] develops the imagery through the names of Viola, Poppy and Rose, later modified to Vi, Flo and Ru, and in the women's costumes which reflect the colours of faded flowers: dull violet, dull red and dull yellow. Ru's name recalls Ophelia's flower-distributing speech in *Hamlet* and Vi, originally called Viola, not only evokes the violet flower, but may recall Viola in *Twelfth Night*, who 'had a sister' pining from unrequited love. Yet there are also other references which counter the fragility of the flower references. Hersch Zeifman points out the reference to the 'Weird Sisters' of *Macbeth* in the first line and compares the three figures to the Fates: 'another trio of sisters, spinning out the web of their life and pondering their destiny'.[44]

These associations work against the individualizing of the three figures, reinforced through the visual appearance of the three and the repetition of their lines, which echo each other. The figures are costumed alike in full-length dresses and wide-brimmed hats. While they are each associated with a particular colour, these are all muted, indeed in his own Paris production, following that of Jean-Marie Serreau in 1966, Beckett removed the colours and substituted shades of grey. In the 1978 Berlin production, each figure wore one item of each colour, undermining any 'colour-specific' identity. The three sequences referring to the absent third's affliction mirror each other although the actual phrasing is different in each case: the French text emphasizes this by substituting three different phrases for the three 'Oh's of the English, but all beginning with M – 'Miséricorde', 'Malheur' and 'Misère'.

The notion of identities dissolving in the face of a common fate is figured in the closing image of the chain formed by the three interlocked pairs of hands. The rings of the chain may also be an image of the undifferentiated void which awaits the three: 'When the three clasp hands at the end, the unbroken chain they form becomes an ironic emblem of eternity.'[45] The predominant image of text and stage, an image which constitutes the figure's past and present, therefore condenses a characteristically dual view of time, suggesting both the temporal process of fading and the transience of the individual before the immense perspective of the endless cycles of time. As James Knowlson points out: 'both the theme and the dramatic structure of the play are dominated by images of circularity and recurrence.'[46]

The text of *Come and Go* is composed almost entirely of refrains and the movements are strictly regular: the noiseless exit, the shifting of positions on the bench, the leaning over to whisper in the other's ear, the significant look, the finger to the lips. The repetition of these gestures traces a pattern which, like a piece of sculpture, draws attention to the space around it. According to Ruby Cohn, discussing Beckett's own Paris production: 'Beckett slowed the playing time from three to seven minutes, so that each gesture seemed wrested from silence.'[47] Likewise the text, which consists of short, recurring phrases, punctuated by pauses, tends to emphasize the silence which the words barely disturb.

This tendency to use words, gesture and movement to evoke spaces and silences is paralleled by the use of lighting. Rather than a bright spotlight defining a particular form against the darkness, *Come and Go*, inspired perhaps by *Krapp's Last Tape*, uses zones of light and dark. The figures are enclosed in a soft circle of light, while the rest of the stage is as dark as possible. Like Krapp, the figures move in and out of this zone of light. Their movements, however, are highly stylized and their feet make no sound. Beckett notes that they should not be seen to leave the stage. The emphasis is simply on their coming and going from the zone of light, a movement which, in the pattern of its recurrence, suggests a perspective in which their own existences are as brief as their stage appearances. As Hersch Zeifman suggests: 'When each of the women in turn leaves the light and disappears into the darkness, we see acted out in that symbolic movement what is simultaneously being whispered about her. The verbal death verdict is thus translated into visual terms – a "going hence".'[48]

The softness of the light also emphasizes the lack of definition characteristic of the play. The dominance of the surrounding dark underlines the visual fragility and insubstantiality of the figures, as does the fact that they make no sound. They seem to occupy some provisional state between absence and presence, darkness and light. The interpenetration of dark and light is suggested by the crossing and recrossing of the zones by the figures and the softness of the circle of light defining the seated figures. Although the published text of *Come and Go* indicates the use of a curtain, subsequent productions have relied upon the by-now characteristic Beckettian technique of the fade-in and fade-out, the gradual transition of the image from appearance to oblivion: 'To frame the dramatic object in this way is to consign it simultaneously to both realms – to make it a kind of visual "ghost," caught in its emergence from one perceptual world to another, wandering in the middle registers of light.'[49]

Visual ghosts is an apt description of the stage images of Beckett's plays of the late 1970s and the 1980s, which reveal an increasing preoccupation with the realms of perceptual and ontological indeterminacy and with the notion of 'between zones'. In *Footfalls*, *Rockaby* and *Ohio Impromptu*, Beckett again explores experiences of absence and loss and how to represent those experiences. These are among Beckett's most poetic plays, as their subjects assume an authority based not on power, judgement and punishment, but on the imaginative generation of comfort and company.

4

REFIGURING AUTHORITY

In the experience of losing another human being whom one has loved, Freud argues, the ego is said to incorporate that other into the very structure of the ego, taking on attributes of the other and 'sustaining' the other through magical acts of imitation. The loss of the other whom one desires and loves is overcome through a specific act of identification that seeks to harbor that other within the very structure of the self.[1]

This schema [the three-dimensional figure of a torus] expresses the endless circularity of the dialectical process that is produced when the subject brings [his] solitude to realisation, be it in the vital ambiguity of immediate desire or in the full assumption of [his] being-for-death.[2]

While the plays considered in the last two chapters focused on a loss of the other's presence, or on a loss of self-presence, the three plays considered in this chapter present the relation between self and an other, although this other may be generated by the self. Rather than figuring the possibility of relationship to an other whose difference from the self is acknowledged, these plays explore ways of achieving comfort for the loss of a loved other through symbolization. These plays therefore confirm the loss of relation to the other as a central personal and cultural crisis and present the recreation of the other through imaginary or narrative means as a source of comfort. Judith Butler refers to the work of Abraham and Torok on introjection and incorporation as responses to loss.[3]

Incorporation [is] a state of disavowed or suspended grief in which the object is magically sustained 'in the body' in some way. . . . Introjection of the loss characteristic of mourning establishes an empty space, literalized by the empty mouth which becomes the condition of speech and signification. The successful displacement of the libido from the lost object is achieved through the formation of words which both signify and displace that object.[4]

The plays investigated in this section are directly concerned with responding to loss through the formation of words. Words both displace the other and produce an other – loss is both avowed and, in *Rockaby* and *Ohio Impromptu*, resolved through the figural or literal restoration of the other. In all three plays, the absence or loss of a desired object during the protagonist's life is countered by the (magical) presence of an other voice/body – the 'another like herself' sought by the subject in *Rockaby*.[5] The restored other in *Footfalls* and *Rockaby* is the lost object of original desire, the Mother.

The relationship between mother and daughter is one which, Irigaray points out, is hardly recognized in patriarchal culture, largely because this culture does not recognize the difference between mother and daughter.[6] While the daughter, under Oedipal law, must transfer her libido from the Mother to an object of the opposite sex, she is culturally identified with the Mother. Hence, Jessica Benjamin writes that 'Woman always speaks with the mother, man speaks in her absence'.[7] Both *Footfalls* and *Rockaby* reproduce such a lack of difference between mother and daughter. As in *Not I*, Beckett is drawing on the feminine to explore areas excluded from dominant patriarchal culture, in particular, the original symbiotic relationship with the Mother, which is repressed in order for self-individuation to take place. The restoration of this fluid relationship between self and other has considerable implications for the concept of authorship, since the authority (however illusory) granted to the self through the signifying position is displaced and dissolved through the relation to the other.

I have chosen to end with *Ohio Impromptu*, not only because it is chronologically later than the other two, but because it reflects directly on the processes of authorship. The other restored in *Ohio Impromptu* is not the Mother, but a brother self. The shadow of the father is also present in this play, both through the initially authoritative relation between Listener and Reader and through the implicit textual references to the figure of James Joyce, with whom Beckett frequently strolled along the Isle of Swans. Through the performance of the play, during which the text is read from a book on the table between the two figures, this relation of authority is transformed into one of fraternity – 'they grew to be as one'. Interestingly, the gender of the loved one in the text, with whom the protagonist once lived, is not specified, but any difference of feature or gender is erased in the identical other who is (at least provisionally) present on stage.[8] *Ohio Impromptu* therefore brings into play a number of levels of identity and relation, which confuse and diffuse questions of authority and authorship. Therefore, unlike Freud's interpretation of the fort/da game as the child's attempt to master loss through figuration, these plays present border zones between self and other, loss and comfort, even between life and death. They therefore represent a development in Beckett's exploration of those areas which elude the dominant structures of symbolic representation, and of how to present such liminal spaces and provisional identities on stage.

FOOTFALLS: DREADFULLY UN-

Footfalls is said to have been inspired by one of Jung's lectures which Beckett attended in the 1920s. Jung was speaking of a female patient and he described her condition as 'never having been really born'.[9] May's struggle with words emphasizes that her lack of identity is also an inability to figure herself as a substantial presence in representation. The Mother's voice is elicited or intervenes as an aid to authorship, but the evocation of her presence only reinforces the experience of her loss. *Footfalls* therefore explores and challenges the borders and limits of identity and presence, foregrounding the intermediary zones between self and other, presence and absence. These metaphysical preoccupations are materialized, however, in Beckett's presentation of perceptual gradations between the seen and the unseen, the heard and the unheard. Indeed, while both the verbal text and the *mise-en-scène* are rigorously structured, the construction of pattern, paralleled by May's attempt to construct a representation of herself, is challenged by the dynamic of the echo, which progressively undermines any fixed forms or constructs in the play.

Beckett has stressed that the text was envisaged from the beginning in relation to the scenic context. During rehearsals for the Berlin production, he emphasized:

the importance of the foot-steps. The walking up and down is the central image, he says. This was my basic conception of the play. The text, the words were only built up around this picture.[10]

However, during the process of composition revealed by the series of manuscripts, the stage directions become more specific, as details about May's appearance, the lighting or sounds in the play are included, and the structure of the verbal text becomes tighter, particularly in the first two sections, composed, as S. E. Gontarski has indicated, before the 'sequel'.[11] Many of the details – particularly in V.'s monologue, the references to the family practitioner who 'fooled [May] into this world', for example – are eliminated in the later versions, while other more suggestive references, to the agony of Christ or the images of coldness, in May's monologue are added.

The increased patterning of the text through verbal and rhythmic repetitions both de-familiarizes the dialogue, so that it sounds less naturalistic, and sets up a play of references between speeches or sections which extends the range of possible meanings. There is a corresponding shift from denotation to connotation – a 'deep sleep', for example, with its evocation of death, the connotations of warmth in 'warming pan' or the many references to cold in the third section: the north door, the adjective 'frozen' or the name Mrs Winter. Indeed, as the text becomes more patterned, meaning itself is destabilized, as there is a continual shift from one level of meaning to another. The references to Christ's agony introduce an immense time perspective and also place the individual within a universal context of suffering. There is therefore a widening of perspective, from the 'here and now' of the stage and the referential denotations of the text which create a specific context – the death-scene of the Mother with pillows and bed-pans, the 'old home' once carpeted or the dining-table scene in the third section – to the much more abstract and unlimited imaginative space created through the play of meanings or connotations.

On the other hand, the verbal patterns stress the materiality of the spoken text as a structure of sounds, so that we are distanced from the play of meanings even as they are offered. Thus, while there is an expansion of possible meanings, there is also a converse movement, a contraction of the very possibility of meaning, as language becomes opaque, focusing in upon the moment of utter-

94

ance in the stage present. Indeed, myth or meaning appear to have no existence outside of the system of language itself. The focus therefore continually shifts from the images evoked in the text to the speaker who is producing them, and to the relationship between the speaking subject, the voice and the language-material she is using. Keir Elam describes this process in relation to *Not I*:

> Such sonic patterns are not simply 'poetic' effects, optional decorative extras lending the monologue an external textual dignity. They serve, above all, to *materialize* the speech continuum (or, in Mouth's case, discontinuum) and thus to foreground the *phoné* itself as stage 'presence' or indeed as theatrical event. In a play like *Not I*, whose efficiency depends in large measure on the voice in its physical as well as narrational qualities, this 'embodying' of discourse is indispensible (Beckett's 'fundamental sounds' again).[12]

The emphasis on repetition, rhythm and pattern also challenges any narrative progression in the play – any attempt to link the sections in a linear or narrative way. The focus is rather on the spatial relationships throughout the performance, in particular, the relationship between the figure May and the voice V.

After the initial chime, echoes and fade-up, the opening image is that of May pacing, which continues for three lengths before the dialogue begins. Her pose, arms tightly clasped around her, stresses her self-enclosure: 'May is there exclusively for herself. She is isolated.'[13] This self-absorption is underlined by her constant retracing of the narrow path described by her pacing, which circumscribes the space of her actions. Her movements are strictly limited to the path of steps and she never moves outside the confines of this space, until the final section, when she has vanished completely, leaving an empty strip of light. This lighted strip which constitutes the pacing area separates May's space of play from the rest of the stage and sets up a series of dualities between light and dark, movement and stillness, inhabited space and uninhabited space. The initiation of the dialogue, however, changes the relationship between the figure and the stage space: the darkness is now animated by the voice and May enters into relationship with this other space – the space of the (M)other.

Beckett deliberately problematizes the relationship between text and stage by emphasizing the ambiguity of the stage space. The fact that V is aroused by May from a 'deep sleep' could suggest that the scene is a past memory being replayed in the present, in May's 'poor mind', the deep sleep suggesting not only, literally, the sleep of the body, but, metaphorically, the depths of memory or death. The lack of specific décor enables the stage space to represent simultaneously a mimetic external space and an internal, subjective space. Indeed, if the scene is being played out in the mind, it may as well be an entirely imagined or fictional scene as a remembered one. The dialogue may be simply the playing out of the *roles* of mother and daughter. Hence the audience's construction of the scene is undermined, as the textual or scenic 'frames' through which they perceive and categorize information are continually shifting, preventing any attempt to recreate a coherent universe. If the play offers us no 'authorized' interpretation, it also challenges the audience's authority, preventing her/him from imposing an interpretation upon it.

All that can be verified, then, in *Footfalls*, is the two subject positions of May and V, each of whom casts the other as object – first and second person pronouns recur throughout the dialogue. The relationship between the two is also ambiguous. On the one hand, May's existence seems to be dependent on that of the Mother. This dependence comes across both in the content or images of the dialogue, where May's life seems devoted to her ailing mother, and in the way each posits herself in language. The Mother asserts or 'owns' her existence (and that of May) within language:

> V: I had you late. (*Pause*) In life.
>
> (p. 240)

No possessives, however, are used to describe May's existence – it is simply 'it all'. The Mother is therefore associated with authority – in relation to language and in relation to May. Yet the notion of origin as the foundation of identity (or authority) is undermined in *Footfalls*, as it was in *A Piece of Monologue*. If May's existence is merely a derivative of that of the Mother, that of the Mother may be created or recreated by May, in which case, the voice is simply the echo of an original presence, and May, the ghost of an echo. The following two sections further undermine any assumption of narrative continuity or of the stable contours or confines of self. What emerges is a process similar to Julia Kristeva's description of Bakhtin's polyphonic discourse, where language is:

as it were, distributed over the various instances of discourse that a multiple 'I' can occupy simultaneously. Appearing first in dialogue form, for we can hear it in the voice of the 'other', the person addressed, it then becomes profoundly polyphonic, for in the end, several instances of discourse become audible. . . . It is the division of the language-user, divided firstly because it is made up of other self, only to become in the end, his own otherness, and therefore multiple and elusive, polyphonic.[14]

This movement from dialogue to polyphony is paralleled in *Footfalls*. The play sets up a series of binary oppositions: self/(M)other, sound/silence, visible/invisible, but proceeds to undermine or blur such divisions, which shatter and multiply into an elusive, shifting spectrum.

The Voice's monologue in Section II underlines the lack of narrative continuity between the two sections. Although the voice is recognizably that of the Mother, her opening phrase ascertains that she is no longer on a death-bed 'V: I walk here now'. Neither of the deictic terms 'here' or 'now' can be related back to the previous scene. The emphasis seems, rather, to be simply on the stage present, as V comments on May's pacing. Yet the boundaries between past and present are eroded throughout Voice's monologue. As well as focusing visually on May in the present, Voice's verbal description evokes a precise spatial location in which her pacing is situated: 'the old home', as well as the temporal perspective of May's past – which can be reduced to a repetition of the same ritual pacing since childhood. The temporal location of the scene is thus ambiguous, as it could be the representation of a past scene, of a present scene observed or imagined by the Mother or simply the 'here and now' of the stage, where the audience watch an actress pacing the boards. The borders between past and present, representation and presentation become shifting and ambiguous.

This section also develops the ambiguity between May and V. While V describes May as pacing up and down the floor of the 'old home', she does not place herself within or in relation to the referential space she creates for and around May. Beckett emphasized the spatial ambivalence of the voice in this section by suggesting in his notebook for the Berlin production that the voice should issue from a localized speaker situated backstage in the first sec-

97

tion, but be delocalized in the second, using, for example, one or two of the speakers used for the German production of *That Time* on the same programme. During this section, therefore, the voice seems to fill the stage space, dominating it, while May is completely closed in upon herself. There is no dialogue between them. In both notebooks (for the Royal Court and for the Schiller-Theater productions) Beckett specifies that May should murmur to herself during this section, in contrast to the previous one, where she listened attentively to V.

The shift in spatial relationship is paralleled by a shift in subject/object positions. In the first section there was a certain complementarity, where each subject also confirmed the other as object. In the second, however, the subject/object positions are more polarized. We have no access to May's subjectivity – she is silent and self-absorbed. V, on the other hand, deliberately posits herself as subject:

> V: I walk here now. (*Pause.*) Rather I come and stand.

She also confirms May as her, and the audience's, object of perception:

> V: But let us watch her move, in silence (*M. paces. Towards end of second length.*) Watch how feat she wheels.
>
> (p. 241)

The collective imperative is misleading, however, as it suggests that the spectator's perception of the scene is identical to the perception of it offered by the voice. While the spectator aurally perceives the description of the old home, her/his vision registers only its absence. Moreover, the spectator's perception is not only focused on May, but on the aural presence of the voice, which tends to dominate the dim visual presence of the figure, particularly as Voice seems to directly address the audience, while May turns in upon herself. There is again a dual focus: on the images evoked in the text and on the relationship between figure and voice on stage. For despite their spatial disparity, the process in which the voice is engaged is precisely that which she attributes to May:

> V: Still speak? Yes, some nights she does, when she fancies none can hear. (*Pause.*) Tells how it was. (*Pause.*) Tries to tell how it was.

Moreover, if Voice's opening words are irreconcilable with her role in the previous section, that is largely because she now appears to be liberated from all confines of space and time. In other words, she may be taken for an unseen ghost, herself sometimes pacing sometimes still, at nightfall. This, however, is precisely what the audience sees before them in the *image* of May. It is as if we are given two perspectives of the same process, or rather of supposedly simultaneous processes, firstly, the visual image of the process of pacing, and secondly, the verbal process of telling how it was, reproduced by the voice.[15] Despite their spatial separation, therefore, the notion of May and V as separate identities is even more radically questioned. In this section, Voice does not specifically identify itself as May's mother. Rather it plays the *role* of mother: firstly in the dialogue within the monologue, where V adopts the roles of both May and Mother, and secondly, V fulfills the function of mother, since she creates May's life in words, tells how it was, a Mother–Author. Yet, as we have seen, this creator is herself perhaps created or projected by May. If one is the origin of the other, no centre is designated: the one reflects the other, like a dialogue of echoes. The very notion of an origin or original/authorial voice is thus progressively undermined.

In the third section, the voice is silent, the darkness no longer animated. May is on her own. There is a corresponding shift in the spatial dynamics of the stage. Rather than the whole stage space constituting the site of the self/(M)other confrontations, May herself becomes the locus of these conflicts/dialogues. For May now attempts to become a Mother–Author herself, and gives birth to as shadowy a creature as herself (formed from her 'given' name, as Amy is an anagram of May) – the ghost child of a ghost child. The pacing figure in May's monologue parallels May herself, the May/Amy relationship evoking the ambiguity of identity and difference between May and Voice and between May and the description of her in Voice's monologue. The image of a dimly lit pacing figure is thus caught up in a series of reflections between the figure on stage, Voice's monologue, where it is placed in the context of the old home, and May's epilogue, where the figure is specifically referred to as a ghost:

A little later, when she was quite forgotten, she began to – (*Pause.*) A little later, when as though she had never been, it never been, she began to walk. (*Pause.*) At nightfall. (*Pause.*)

Slip out at nightfall and into the little church by the north door, always locked at that hour, and walk, up and down, up and down, his poor arm.

(p. 242)

The initial dialogue between May and Voice now diverges further to become a chorus of echoes. The pacing figure in May's monologue parallels May herself, and the symmetry between the two monologues, and particularly between the two dialogues within the monologues, suggests that 'Amy' is a younger version of Voice's May, just as the May of Voice's dialogue scene appears to be a younger version of May herself. The Amy/Mrs Winter dialogue thus mirrors the May/Mother dialogue, itself an echo of the first dialogue between May and V. During rehearsals for the Berlin production in 1976, Walter Asmus reports that Beckett particularly wanted to emphasize:

the similarity between daughter and mother. 'The daughter only knows the voice of the mother.' One can recognize the similarity between the two from the sentences in their narratives, from the expression. The strange voice of the daughter comes from the mother. The 'Not enough?' in the mother's story must sound just like the 'Not there?' of Mrs W. in Amy's story, for example.[16]

Yet the echoes also cut across these mother/daughter couples, as the image of the ghost pacing not only links May with Amy, but these daughter figures with the image of V/Mother in the opening words of the second section. The binary divisions between daughter/mother, self/other, author/fictional creation therefore become increasingly blurred. All that is left in the third section is a ghost-like echo composed of other echoes, condemned to a cycle of repetition until it finally fades completely into silence and absence in the fourth section. It is interesting to note that the first two sections of the original manuscript are labelled by Beckett 'A: Dying Mother B: Mother back', paralleling the previously mentioned fort/da ritual observed by Freud, where the child attempts to come to terms with the loss of the Mother's presence by 'staging' that loss.

The preoccupation with echoes, and the questioning of the Voice as original source, therefore reflect a Derridean displacement of presence as the centre of all thought and being, which perpetuates the multiplication of echoes. Yet, through the references to the Mother, the stage space in *Footfalls* also evokes, as in *Not I*, the maternal body from which May has never emerged. Her 'never having been born' could therefore refer not only to her lack of presence, but to her inability to separate herself from the Mother.

Indeed, the stage space seems to shift from the contained, internal space of the womb, where the divisions between self and other are fluid, and which is, in a sense, the 'space' of the Mother's voice, to the unbounded space of infinite loss and absence in the third section when the Mother's voice no longer animates the external space of the stage, although it haunts May's discourse. The third section is, as previously mentioned, associated with images of coldness, in contrast to the 'warming pan' in the first section. If the loss of original (paternal/maternal) presence multiplies the play of signification and identity, the loss of the Mother's body/voice chains the subject to the perpetual repetition of the staging of that loss. There is indeed no mastery in *Footfalls*, only the repetition of increasing cycles of loss. This lack of being or presence is not only revealed through the pattern of the dialogue, but pervades the entire perceptual structure of the play. For *Footfalls* also challenges the oft-quoted Berkeleyan dictum 'Esse est percipi'. If the voice becomes an echo, the appearance becomes a shadow: 'the semblance'.

For May's visual presence is also undermined. The stage image is juxtaposed with represented images in the text which are *not* present(ed) on stage: the old home or the locked church. During the dialogue in Voice's monologue, May is identified with her past (absent) self. Moreover, in the third section, the visual image of May parallels the entirely fictional and, by definition, ontologically ambiguous ghost of Amy. Every level of given reality is problematized. The very image of May is more shadow than substance. The lighting, dim and cold, is strongest at floor level, faintest at the head, though a spot on the face is added during May's monologue. Hence, like the figure in *A Piece of Monologue*, the emphasis is on May's appearance as visual *material*, rather than on her physical presence. Peter Gidal notes:

> The figure on stage in *Footfalls*, wrapped, is never a figure inside a wrap. It is, as a whole, a wrap.[17]

Indeed, within May's monologue, she is implicitly identified with Amy, who denies her own presence. In a sense May also denies her presence, by representing herself in the third person, as 'not I'. Presentation, the indication that something 'is there', is progressively replaced by representation – the semblance of the original.

Attention is continually drawn to the perceptual qualities of the verbal and scenic material in the play. The text emphasizes the activities of seeing and hearing: V seems to exist mainly to hear May in the first section and to see her in the second. The audience are thus made aware of their own perceptual experience of the play. The momentum of the play would therefore seem to be the production of self: the rhythm of birth, at which the audience assists . . . like a mid-wife. Yet, instead of rising towards completion or creation, the rhythm increasingly loses momentum and simply fades out. By the third section, all perception has become fainter and more problematical. The pacing figure in May's monologue makes no sound that can be heard and is only visible in a certain light. This deterioration in perceptual quality is reflected in the stage image where the light is dimmer, the image fainter and the voice softer. The audience is thus implicated in the *failure* of production (or self-individuation) which becomes rather the repetition of a never-completed labour. If there is no origin in *Footfalls*, there is likewise no ending, neither birth nor death, but some in-between state, some womb/tomb space occupied by the unborn and the undead – shades caught between the definitive contours of form or identity and the formless infinity of space.

The main dramatic tension in *Footfalls* is therefore not the momentum of birth, but the inexorable pattern of repetition:

V: Will you never have done. (*Pause.*) Will you never have done revolving it all?

The emphasis thus shifts from the representation of self to the process of representing. The visual image fails to either present or represent May (a representation is defined by Barthes in 'Diderot, Brecht, Eisenstein' as an image which is clearly defined 'découpé' which the image of May is not)[18] but focuses rather on the sounds which she produces. The light is strongest at floor level but we do not see the feet, the stage directions emphasize that the feet should not be visible, therefore the entire emphasis is on the sound and pattern of the footfalls. The production of self is set against the production of pattern: if being or lack of being cannot be figured, at least some shape or pattern, however faint, can be traced against the void.

The task of self-production is also set within the wider framework of the technical production of the play itself. Again, the pattern of the scenic text is foregrounded. Beckett's production notebooks develop the exact timing of each element of sound or lighting: the chime with echoes, the fade-ups and fade-outs all last seven seconds; the three sections should each last five minutes, with the fourth lasting again seven seconds. As James Knowlson underlines, the repetition of this pattern before and after each 'act' of the play, emphasizes the gradual diminution of all the perceptual elements:

> The form of the play therefore becomes that of a series of circular revolutions, moving from one phase of absence to another, gradually fading away into less and less sharp definition and moving towards silence, stillness, and deepening darkness.[19]

While this scenic pattern 'frames' the spoken text, it also shifts attention from the 'staging of self' to the more abstract pattern of the play as a whole, in which May or Voice can be considered as visual or aural elements. The play thus also denies itself as representation, a final self-negation summarized by the play's French title, *Pas*, presenting itself simply as pattern, constructed upon, indeed from, 'unfathomable abysses of silence'. Peter Gidal has pointed out the ambivalence in the play between the acknowledgement of the need to express 'being' and the radical undermining of the representational apparatus which expresses through the psychology of the 'self':

> Nothing is stabilised, not even the imagination's machinations. There is no (illusion) of ego, and without it expressionism cannot function; but the demands of expression are constantly implicated. *It is precisely in that that Beckett's theatre does not abjure the material historical subjectivity of the human figure, speech, movement, but rather, uses it radically, against individualism, against expressionism, and against the reproduction of given identities.*[20]

ROCKABY: THOSE ARMS AT LAST

In both *Rockaby* and *Ohio Impromptu* the speaking of the text becomes a rite of passage which enacts a transformation – from loss to comfort, from life to death and from speech to silence. In both plays the ritual is concerned with the reconciliation of difference, with bringing an end to the continual reproduction of the cycles of self and other, desire and its object, thus enabling the restless dynamic of desire to be laid to rest. I have already referred to Kristeva's concept of the *chora* or maternal body in *Revolution in Poetic Language* which she sees as a dynamic space where differences exist without duality and where the subject is caught up in the continual processes of construction and destruction. This rhythmic energy constitutes a subversive force which repeatedly launches its assaults upon the traditional structures and boundaries of the Symbolic. However, Kristeva also associated the *chora* with the Freudian death-drive, through the interaction within the *chora* of the rhythm of the pulsions, and moments of temporary stasis, anticipating the final stasis of death: 'The semiotic chora, converting drive discharges into stases, can be thought of both as a delaying of the death drive and as a possible realization of this drive, which tends to return to a homeostatic state.'[21] The Mother's body remains the site where difference is reconciled, but instead of being embraced in a process where difference is endlessly produced and dissolved, the maternal body is both restored as the original lost object and provides a space where the reconciliation of difference may be imaginatively realized or at least rehearsed.

Rockaby recalls the rhythms of the *chora* in its 'nonchronological, repetitious, spiralling, cumulative, fluid language',[22] yet it also presents the Mother as harbour and harbinger of death. The evocation of a ritualized movement of contraction and descent seems to reflect a return to the womb and the soothing quality of the voice seems to seduce the daughter into death, as her image fuses with that of her dead/dying mother. *Ohio Impromptu* also focuses on a ritual of narration, which creates a space of fiction or fictional space in which the boundaries between self and other, author and fictional creature, the subject and his death are eroded. Rather than cycles of emprisonment or torture, these plays present the processes of fiction as a source or at least a shade of comfort.

On one level, *Rockaby* tells the story of an old woman approaching and entering death after a long and lonely existence. As Hersch

Zeifman has noted: '. . . we see a woman, rocking away, listening to a tale – a tale that is narrated rather than dramatised.'[23] However, as Zeifman also points out, this narrative is placed within a scenic context which, as in *Ohio Impromptu* written the next year, focuses on the production and perception of the life-story told by the text. Both scenic and textual levels, however, contrast the repetition or reproduction of the parallel processes of existence and the telling or representation of that existence with the desire to cease both being and telling, expressed simultaneously within the narrative and by the figure on stage:

time she stopped
time she stopped

The narrative summarizes its subject's existence as a perpetual search for an other:

all eyes
all sides
high and low
for another

The desired other, however, is an other 'like' the self, whose need in turn for an other would reflect the need of the self:

for another
another like herself
another creature like herself
a little like
going to and fro
all eyes
all sides

The desire to perceive the other seems to be the desire for a reflection of the self, or rather, the desire to recognize the desire of the 'self' in the desire of the other. Should this other be found, the need of each, instead of circulating endlessly, would respond to the other, each becoming simultaneously subject and object of desire in a completed cycle, as in the final image of *Ohio Impromptu* where 'the moment of self-recognition consummates the union of the self with itself in the mirror of the other'.[24]

The subject in the first sections of the narrative is identified only with the eyes, the only part of her body which is mentioned. Indeed, she seems to have no existence beyond her need to see and recognize the other, which condemns her to a ceaseless wandering in search of her object. The desire of the subject of the narrative to see the other is mirrored by the desire of the figure to hear her own life-story. Although the figure does not control the voice,[25] the four sections of the narrative and the accompanying motion of the rocker are preceded by the four imploring 'More's uttered by the figure. In *Rockaby*, this desire is not only narrated in the text and suggested in the scenic figure's utterances, but is materialized in the structure and rhythm of the performance. The repeated motion of the search within the text is reflected in the rhythm of the recorded narrative, indeed its form counters its status as narrative, associated traditionally with the linear development of the plot. The text is divided into short rhythmic units, synchronous with the rocking of the chair. Each section contains a limited number of these units which are continually repeated, with each new unit woven into the cycle of repetitions. Each of the four sections repeats in large measure the previous one(s), but adds a number of new phrases which develop the story or narrative while maintaining the circular, repetitive rhythm. Jane Hale has compared the form of the text to:

> the repetitive narrative songs that seem to be coming to an end, only to recommence at the beginning in an endless game of mirrors
>
> (p. 133)

The motion of repetition becomes the very rhythm of desire, the 'spirals of need' referred to by Beckett in his article on Denis Devlin's *Intercessions* or the repetition of the child's game in Freud's 'Beyond the Pleasure Principle'. The need of the subject of the narrative for the other becomes the need to represent her need, the need to hear the history of her need. While need persists, however, the history can never be completed, but only renewed or repeated. The desire to end is therefore the desire to end the 'compulsion to repeat', the desire to end desiring, since the repetition can only cease when need itself, the animating principle, is laid to rest. The elimination of need, however, entails the elimination of the duality of the concepts of self and other, need and its object. Only when this difference or margin which perpetuates the circulation of desire is resolved into union, if not unity, can need be soothed.

Indeed, the dynamic of the play's structure seems to present the reproduction of difference as a function of the processes of representation, as in Lacan, the entry into Language produces the split subject. The existence of the central 'character' in *Rockaby*, as in many other Beckett plays, is constructed through three distinct elements of representation, each of which is played off against the other: the text, which recreates the past or history of the character; the voice; and the visible image of the figure. While these three elements could be taken as different perspectives on a single object or 'signified' – the entity of the old woman – such an interpretation is countered by the presentation of each layer of scenic or textual representation as produced fiction.

As Charles Lyons has argued, the narrative of the old woman's past is unverifiable as history and its presentation as spoken monologue tends to foreground its nature as a recited text:

> The past has presence for the character only as a verbal structure that revolves in consciousness.[26]

Indeed, because of the particularly repetitive nature of the text, it tends to dissolve into the pure sound or rhythm of the voice. Moreover, by using the technique of the recorded voice, attention is drawn to the voice itself as produced material. Enoch Brater notes that 'its eerie tone, modulated but always metallic, is never entirely human'.[27]

In contrast to *Footfalls*, where the figure of May was little more than a shadow, the image of the old woman is perfectly visible, indeed almost baroque by the standard of most of the later plays:

> *Black lacy high-necked evening gown. Long sleeves. Jet sequins to glitter when rocking. Incongruous flimsy head-dress set askew with extravagant trimming to catch light when rocking.*

> (p. 273)

However, the very stress on visibility presents the image as visual material. The fade-up of the light emphasizes the constructed quality of the image: only the face is revealed at first, then, after a long pause, the rest of the body, seated in the chair, emerges from the dark. The image as a whole suggests confinement and enclosure, the materiality of the inanimate. The only parts of the body exposed are the face and the hands, and these, in their whiteness and immobility, seem closer to the material than to the human. Whiteness and pallor also suggest death and, except when the large staring eyes are open, the face, with its deep shadows, looks almost already a death-mask. The rest of the body is entirely enclosed within the full-length, high-necked, long-sleeved costume, in turn encased in the wooden form of the rocking chair, whose arms encircle the figure 'to suggest embrace'.

The fixity or materiality of the image is countered, however, by the mobile elements of the performance. The rhythm of the rocking and the continual play of the light over the sequins and the polished wood of the chair endow the image with what Brater describes as a 'kinetic' quality. In the stage directions, Beckett suggests that the main spot may be focused on the head at rest, so that during the performance the head and the body are constantly moving in and out of light:

> Beckett in fact makes us see the same figure in different artificial lights, offering us an ever-shifting series of perspectives from which to encounter the image anew.[28]

Again, the emphasis shifts from the materiality of the image as 'object' to the processes of perception, since, as Brater notes, their object remains elusive. Indeed, shape or form, whether narrative, voice or visual image, is never 'given' but is constructed and maintained in a series of diminishing cycles of desire, representation and perception which constitute the dynamic structure of the play.

Indeed, the structure of *Rockaby* can be seen as the juxtaposition of two impulses or rhythms: on the one hand, the continual repetition of the series or cycles of need/representation/perception, reflected in the to and fro movement which pervades the play; and on the other hand, the movement of diminution, withdrawal and descent, the fading, as in *Footfalls*, of the perceptual elements of the play and the retraction of the cycles of repetition ever closer to this still centre which is the end or absence of need, representation and perception. The problem remains, however, of how to escape, once and for all, the self-perpetuating cycles of representation. As Charles Lyons argues:

> Beckett's characters are confined both within some restrictive space and within the limits of a text that revolves in their imagination.[29]

In both *Rockaby* and *Ohio Impromptu*, however, it is precisely the repetition of this text that acts as the transition or ritual out of need, out of Time and out of self (and other). By producing an other 'like' the self, the other who is different but the same, in

Rockaby the image of the Mother and in *Ohio Impromptu* a manifestly identical other (brother ?) self (an other inseparable from the text, an apparitional counterpart), the text attempts to heal the wound of difference and desire.

On a number of different levels throughout the play, difference, duality and repetition (associated with Time) are contrasted with the contrary impulse towards synchronicity, union and closure. This is not only effected in the images of self and other/mother figured in the text, but also in the relationship between text and stage. At the beginning of the performance, the spatio-temporal frame of the narrative contrasts strongly with that of the stage present. The visual image is confined to a small area of the stage, while the first section of the narrative evokes an external, uncircumscribed and unlimited zone of space and time traversed by the subject, wandering in all directions, high and low, to and fro, in search of the other. There are no stable visual references, the entire emphasis is on the dispersed motion of the search. No direct mention is made of the subject's body, only of the eyes, so that the physical motion of the quest condenses into the searching gaze of the eyes (as the body in *Not I* condenses and dissolves into the stream of speech uttered by Mouth):

> all eyes
> all sides

In the second section, the centrifugal and dispersed motion of the search in all directions is countered by the impulse towards withdrawal, as the subject retreats to an internal space whose horizons are limited to a window looking out onto other windows:

> in the end went and sat
> went back in and sat
> at her window
> let up the blind and sat
> quiet at her window
> only window
> facing other windows

(p. 277)

The motion of the search continues in the activity of gazing out of the window, but this motion is increasingly contained within a more passive and confined spatial framework: the boundaries of the room with its single window, at which the woman sits 'quiet'.

109

The shift from a continual motion of displacement to a growing passivity and withdrawal is paralleled by an increasing emphasis on the image of the body: the non-figurable activity of the search becomes the image of the woman at the window, her body finally at rest. Throughout Beckett's work, the room with its window frequently becomes a metaphor for the body and the relationship between the inner and the outer worlds. The withdrawal into the room is therefore also a withdrawal into the body (finally revealed as the maternal body, the initial lost object/other which announces the exile of the subject and his/her essential incompleteness and which is therefore the final resting place and object of desire).

The third section, paralleling the first, focuses again on the search, which is therefore counterpointed with the contrary impulse towards passivity and rest (which dominate the second and fourth sections). Yet a distance has been created between the desiring subject and the outer world in which any other might be encountered. Any direct meeting of famished eyes to famished eyes is now out of the question, as the circulating movement of desire and of the gaze has been replaced by a single (blind) signifier, which would indicate to the subject simply the existence of another buried within like herself:

> never mind a face
> behind the pane
> famished eyes
> like hers
> to see
> be seen

However, when even the sign of another raised blind is denied the subject, she turns her back completely on the outer world and retreats farther into the space within.

The movement of withdrawal and retreat culminates in the image of descending the stairs, penetrating to a confined space, closed off from any other reality. The association of this space with the womb, or maternal body, is reinforced by the references to the mother throughout this final section. In *Rockaby*, as opposed to *Footfalls*, the mother is no longer a lost presence or authority, but emerges finally both as the long-desired other/imago of the desiring self and as the space which *contains* the self, its other and its history. Not only does the image of the daughter merge with

110

that of her mother, preparing for her own death, but the womb-space which contains the rocker is associated with fusion and convergence, instead of the earlier dispersal and alienation.

In this fourth section, stage image and text also begin to converge. The image of the old woman in the arms of the rocker all in black/best black not only merges daughter with mother, but textual description with stage image, so that the convergence occurs on several levels. Temporal movement and spatial stasis are also reconciled within this scene which combines visual image with continual motion, where the futile search for the absent other has become the self-contained motion of the rocker, moving back and forth on its own axis. The beginning is contained within the end, and vice versa, as this womb-space contains both self and mother, and condenses the time-span of the mother's long years in the rocker as well as the life-time of the daughter into a single shifting image (shifting between mother and daughter and between motion and – as yet temporary – stases).

The elements of finery and formality in the costume also evoke and condense the two main ceremonies attending the beginning and ending of life: birth and death. The rocker in turn suggests both cradle and coffin. The touches of incongruous frivolity may also suggest the long-awaited nuptials of self, mother and death. Both figure and rocking-chair are associated with the mother, so that the enclosure of the arms of the rocker is also the embrace of the mother-death. Differences and dualities are not transformed into unity (the One), but are resolved within this fusion of all forms and identities and times and spaces with the mother:

> into the old rocker
> mother rocker
> where mother rocked[30]

The history of need has become an image of comfort, providing the longed-for reflection of like to like.

This reflection is also, however, mirrored in the relationship between rocking figure and voice. Even the voice is associated with the mother through the references to the text as lullaby, already suggested by its soothing musical rhythm and confirmed by the play's title, which in French – 'Berceuse' – means simultaneously rocking-chair, cradle and lullaby, while the English title 'Rockaby' refers to the famous lullaby 'Rockaby baby'. The narration of the search animated by unfulfilled desire becomes the comforting

111

rhythm of the voice, as motion and desire (whether to hear or to see) are gradually quieted. Moreover, the sense of convergence is reflected in the synchronicity between the rhythm of the rocker and the rhythm of the voice: 'one full revolution of her rock encompasses one printed line of verse.'[31] Indeed, as Zeifman has commented, the entire trajectory of the narrative is itself condensed into the fading rhythm and texture of the scenic performance:

> The story V narrates is a lullaby turned threnody, its movement a contraction and descent. . . . On the narrative level, V's monologue is divided into four sections, each section describing a progressive diminution, a cascando, a descent into silence and immobility. And this is precisely what we see and hear dramatized on stage. As the story winds down, so too does the stage picture: narration and theater image coalesce.[32]

The text therefore not only produces the (m)other image of the narrative, and creates a space of fusion and convergence, which enables desire to be soothed, but itself also constitutes the 'mirror', where the subject is reflected back at herself in the third person:

> was her own other
> own other living soul

At the same time, narrative is condensed into voice, into the maternal, seductive other, lulling the subject into the arms of death – 'those arms at last'. As the end approaches, the rhythm gathers into a final effort, the last motions of birth into death, in which time and history, self and other, existence itself are aborted:

> fuck life
> rock her off
> rock her off

With no more desire to reproduce or perceive her history, no more need to see or to tell – 'stop her eyes' – the dynamic of the performance and the existence it represents fades. The voice becomes a dying echo and the motion of the rocker comes to rest. The light narrows in to focus on the head, as it performs the closing motions of an existence, as the head slowly falls forward, then becomes quite still. Only after this is achieved does the light fade completely. The existence of the old woman is therefore both produced and ended through the performance. Yet despite the impulse towards synchronicity during the play, seeing and saying do not end simultaneously. The audience are intensely aware of their own act of seeing, particularly when the light has focused in on the head at the very moment of (simulated) death. On the one hand, the audience are thus made aware of the faculty of perception which persists in order to *see* the moment of ending, as at the end of *Ill Seen Ill Said*.[33] On the other, it confronts the audience both with the boundary of death, which has apparently been crossed, leaving the audience facing a death-mask, and with the masquerade of representation, which can only *simulate* or rehearse death, the ultimate fading of presence. Yet through this ritual of performance an other has been embodied, embracing both self and other, the living and the dead. Beckett's next play, *Ohio Impromptu*, continues the exploration of self and symbolized other. While this play presents two male actors and deals explicitly with questions of authorship, the performance transforms what appears to be a hierarchical relation of authority into one of compassion and comfort.

OHIO IMPROMPTU: RITES OF PASSAGE

Ohio Impromptu is centrally concerned with the processes of creation and with the generation of difference inherent in these processes: creator/creature, listener/speaker, stage/text. *Ohio Impromptu* was originally written in English for an international symposium on 'Samuel Beckett: Humanistic Perspectives' at Ohio State University during May 1981. The title links the play to a theatrical tradition of Impromptus, including Molière's *Impromptu de Versailles*, Giraudoux' *Impromptu de Paris* and Ionesco's *Impromptu de l'Alma*. These, according to Pierre Astier:

> deal to a large extent with problems of play-acting or play-writing through the acting or the writing of a play that turns out to be the very one performed before our eyes.[34]

The work therefore announces iteself as a play about creation and the artistic practice of its author. However, rather than incorporating a personal apologia into the text, Beckett sets up a dialogue between the different levels or languages of the play, in particular between the scenic and the verbal, so that each comments upon the other and together they constitute an 'auto-critique' of the author's work.

In Beckett's later plays, the visual image is largely static, while the spoken text is usually in the form of monologue, or, in *Ohio Impromptu*, narrative, read from a book by one of the figures on stage. These two levels of representation, the scenic and the verbal, are therefore deliberately differentiated to produce a juxtaposition of narrative and visual image. The narrative of *Ohio Impromptu* tells of a loved one lost and subsequently regained, while the scenic level focuses on the reading and reception of the narrative and its relation to the two figures on stage. The play can indeed be seen as a staging of the processes of fictional creation and of auto-biography in particular: the self as creator of fictional selves. Pierre Astier has seen the book in front of the Reader not only as the record of a life, but as constituting:

> a writer's life-work, a whole oeuvre representing in this case, I think, that of Beckett himself in a make-believe compilation of all his writings so far.[35]

The later plays tend to present a single image which remains stamped in the audience's memory – from the three urns in *Play* or Mouth in *Not I*, to the rocking figure in *Rockaby* or the identical white-haired figures bent over the table in *Ohio Impromptu*. However, the dramatic tension in these plays derives from the juxta-position between stage image and narrative, which is usually in the second or third person, emphasizing the displacement of the 'I' from the centre of the narrative. The image, whose mode of existence, as we have seen, is spatial rather than temporal, which almost seems to be beyond Time, like a still life, enabling it to be fixed (a favourite Beckettian verb) in the perceiver's eye, is set against the narrative, which both reconstitutes action in time and reflects the internal 'subjective' emotions or thoughts of the protag-onist.[36] The image in *Ohio Impromptu* certainly constitutes a stable point of reference throughout the performance, but its essentially static nature is undermined, firstly by the gestures, which intro-duce a dynamic element into the stage image and which may affect or even challenge our interpretation of it, and secondly by the continual modification or re-view of the scenic image in the light of the text.

In contrast to most of the preceding plays, where only one human figure or only the fragment of a figure can be seen, the stage image of *Ohio Impromptu* presents two figures seated by a table. Indeed, compared to the fragmentation characteristic of such plays as *Not I* or *That Time*, the image of *Ohio Impromptu* possesses a certain formal completeness – it has been compared to a Rembrandt painting. The white table visually unites the two figures – the elements of the image are not isolated and separated by space like the figure, lamp and pallet in *A Piece of Monologue*. The two figures are identical in costume and pose, seated diagonally opposite each other, across the table. Even the book is complemented by the round, wide-brimmed hat, completing the 'still life'.

In many of the previous plays, Beckett has deliberately 'decentred' the image in terms of stage space. The head in *That Time* is '*off centre*', the Speaker in *A Piece of Monologue* is '*well off centre downstage audience left*' and the rocker in *Rockaby* is '*slightly off centre*'. For *Ohio Impromptu*, however, the table is '*mid-stage*' and our attention is drawn to the centre of the table where the hat is placed. The pattern or rhythm of the visual elements therefore suggests a certain harmony and complementarity, rather than fragmentation and isolation.

On the other hand, however, this reciprocity is founded on the duality which has dominated the structure of Beckett's plays since *Waiting for Godot*. The colour contrast, which in the first two manuscript versions was between black coats and grey hair, is sharpened into black and white. The two figures mirror each other but also confront each other. In the stage directions, Beckett specifies that the chairs be armless, giving a tenser, more upright sitting position, in contrast to *Rockaby*, where the arms of the chair embrace and enclose the body. The diagonal positioning of the figures across the stage expresses this dual tension of difference and identity. Before a word of the text is spoken, the visual image has already established an ambiguous interplay between identity and alterity, separateness and complementarity. The very emphasis on centring in fact underlines the more radical displacement of the centre through the presentation of the dual protagonist.

The relationship between the two figures remains ambiguous and 'open' and our interpretation of it is developed through the series of gestures and through the text. The gestures take the place of dialogue, establishing a relationship between the two figures and between the figures and the text. While the narrative is being read, the static nature of the visual image enables us to concentrate on the images evoked, but the gestures bring us back to the 'here and now' of the stage. They are performed slowly and are highly stylized, investing the stage space like the movements of a Noh dancer. The first lines of the text 'Little is left to tell' – repeated half-way through the narrative, dividing it into two sections – and the phrase 'Nothing is left to tell' at the end, create a framework which identifies the reading or completion of the book with the duration of the performance. The gestures emphasize that the presentation and perception of the narrative is the focus of the scenic level of representation. The two figures are defined in relation to the narrative: Listener and Reader. The gestures foreground these roles and maintain the continual shift of focus from what is told to the conditions of the telling. The Listener's taps, which are the basic gesture repeated throughout the play, structure the reading and suggest that authority rests with him. They also focus on the Listener's response to the text, highlighted during the repetitions, suggesting that he is also the subject of the narrative. This linking of the Listener with the protagonist of the text is reinforced through the description of the latter in the text which identifies him with the figure on stage. The text can thus be seen as the narrative or autobiography of the Listener. The juxtaposition of the scenic and the textual levels, however, creates various levels of ambiguity and raises questions as to the relationship between self and narrated self, between autobiography and fiction, between the narrative and its source.

The gestures also emotionally invest the relationship between Listener and Reader. They create a rhythm through their repetition so that any variation becomes significant. The two departures from the basic pattern of the Listener's taps on the table counter the distance between the two figures established by their pose – heads bowed, not facing each other – and by the apparently authoritative stance of the Listener. Firstly, towards the end of the first section of the text, the Reader interrupts himself to look up a previous reference and his hand is stayed by that of the Listener – a much fuller and more intimate gesture, the hand of the Listener reaching out to touch or almost touch that of the Reader. The second variation is the final gesture when all has been said, and the hands of both figures are lowered simultaneously, while their heads are raised to meet each other's gaze, forming a complete mirror image. The gestures seem to express a growing intimacy, culminating in the final image. They also draw our attention to the Listener's activity of listening and responding to the text. During the repeated phrases in particular, we construct an emotional response towards the text on the Listener's part. There is therefore an evolution in our perception of the stage image. While at first it appears rather formal – its 'formality' emphasized by the symmetry – it gradually becomes emotionally invested through the growing relationship between Listener and Reader and between the narrative and the figures on stage.

While the scenic level concentrates on the relationship between Listener and Reader and between the two figures and the text, the narrative presents two further series of relationships: between the protagonist and the 'loved one' in the first section of the text; and between the protagonist and the 'shade' or reader in the second section. Another set of relationships which crosses the internal and external boundaries of the narrative are implied: that between the departed loved one (in the world beyond) and his representative, the shade, and that between the reader within the narrative and the reader *of* the narrative, the Reader, again poised between identity and difference. Indeed, the entire work can be seen as a multi-levelled structure which, through the juxtaposition of these relationships, establishes a series of dichotomies: self/other, self/fiction (or fictional self), presence/absence, which are linked to an emotional core which is also articulated along a dual axis of division/reunion, isolation/company, exile (or loss)/comfort. Yet there is a continual slippage and counter-reference between these interconnected pairs, initiating a process of metamorphosis which challenges any fixed boundaries which the emphasis on oppositional pairings may at first suggest.

The first section of the text recreates an alternative space and time and another (although identical) protagonist. The two immobile figures within the undefined space and 'present' of the stage are contrasted with the single figure of the textual protagonist, ceaselessly coming and going from interior to exterior, wandering 'Day after day. . . . Hour after hour' along the Isle of Swans, in the recognizable town-scape of Paris. The 'other' is not represented, indeed the images and the action in this first section of the text are founded upon the *absence* of the other, the loved one, in contrast to the dual presence on stage. The representational quality of the narrative is countered, however, by the emotional charge of the words and phrases: 'last attempt to obtain relief', 'so long together', 'him alone'. Rather than signifiers for an external reality, these words or images tend to create a significant 'pattern' which contrasts isolation or exile with the memory of a

117

shared place and time. In Suzanne Langer's terms, they become 'logically expressive forms . . . symbols for the articulation of feeling'.[37]

The first section of the narrative therefore not only tells a tale, presumably of the Listener's past, but also creates a climate of solitude and exile in space and time against which the advent of comfort promised by the 'dear face' achieves its full resonance. The dominant 'motif' of division and reunion is expressed in the image (both prophetic and ironic) of the two streams of the river flowing together: 'How in joyous eddies its two arms conflowed and flowed united on' (p. 286). Apart from the description of the protagonist, linking him with the Listener on stage, and the mention of the 'dear face', this is the only visual image in this section, and it functions almost like a '*mise-en-abyme*' for the series of dual relationships in the play.

Within this landscape of solitude, the occurence of the dream is like an oasis of comfort. In contrast to the protagonist's exile evoked in the first passages of the text, within the dream space divisions of space and time (between the temporal world and the 'other') are transcended, as the protagonist receives a visitation from the deceased loved one. These dreams, however, only accentuate the protagonist's present isolation, to which he has apparently irrevocably committed himself by his move to an unfamiliar place in an attempt to escape the memories of the past. The dream passage is isolated in the centre of the section by two interruptions by the Listener: the first emphasizing the protagonist's turning away from the above-mentioned image of reunion, the second reinforcing the renewed contact with the loved one: 'Seen the dear face and heard the unspoken words, Stay where we were so long alone together, my shade will comfort you' (p. 286).

The final passage of this section evokes a succession of sleepless nights following the dream visitations, as the protagonist now vainly regrets his move away from the shared place. This period of his life connects, indeed merges, with an earlier period of loneliness, creating a sense of an endless series of sleepless nights from which the memory or hope of comfort or company has been excluded: 'White nights now again his portion' (p. 286). The contrast between text and stage is emphasized through the many interruptions during this passage, which continually draw our attention to the stage *present*, in contrast to the absent past, recreated only in the telling. It also draws our attention to the enigma of the 'other self' on stage: the 'schismatic self',[38] the split between voice and listener, perceived and perceiver which dominates the structure of Beckett's plays, though rarely has it been presented as such a visual 'double' on stage. The scenic level therefore concentrates on the process of story-telling, or specifically, the telling of the story of the self. The voice has therefore assumed a body and while the exact status and identity of that body remain ambiguous, it tends to be associated with the text being read. The scenic image can therefore be seen as a materialization of the processes of self-creation represented by the fictional/autobiographical text: the creator creates himself through the narrative, or is created by it (the self being as much a fiction as the fictional self) in a process of scissiparity or schizogenesis presented on stage.

The narrative, however, also presents a fictional self within the text – the protagonist. The relationship between Listener and Reader is paralleled by the relationship between Listener and his textual counterpart, the protagonist. On the one hand, the differences between stage and text, particularly in the alternative endings they present, emphasize the impossibility of complete identification between author and autobiographical self, confirming that:

> the autobiographical self is a fictional construct within the text, which can neither have its origins anterior to the text, nor indeed coalesce with its creator.[39]

On the other hand, during the second section of the narrative there is a growing identification between the text, the tale of being, isolated in space and time and focusing on the relationship between self and other, and the stage image, focusing on the narration and reception of the tale. Rather than representing an absent past, the text is now re-presenting what is already present(ed) on stage. The very relationship between the two is polyvalent. The text can be seen simultaneously as autobiography, fiction (or sum of fictions) and as an alternative version or metaphor for (its own) creation.

The second section of the narrative focuses on the nocturnal space first introduced in the previous section. As in *Nacht und Traume*, the dream is first inserted into a wider frame, then becomes the sole arena in the next section. Within this 'privileged' space the shade of the 'dear face' appears to the protagonist and comforts him by reading from 'a worn volume'. The pervasive sense of loss, even of torment, throughout the previous section highlights the unhoped-for or despaired-of 'grace' of the presence of the shade and his reading to the protagonist. The implicit reference to the Comforter (Holy Spirit or Ghost) sent by Christ to the disciples after his Ascension is central to this section. It widens the notion of Comfort to include both the personal or individual and the transcendent; it also suggests the existence of a space or world beyond the temporal world, which can communicate with it in certain privileged circumstances, either through the form of the Ghost or vision/visitation or, of course, in the Judaeo-Christian tradition, through the Word. Indeed, the sad tale becomes the (hi)story of humankind telling (hi)stories and turning to the word/Word for comfort. The self dissolves into 'all humanity'.[40]

As well as this centrifugal movement, however, there is a contrary tendency summarized by the central line of this section: 'With never a word exchanged they grew to be as one' (p. 287). This single line (composed of two parts) marks the culmination of the emotional articulation or reunion and comfort, transcending the different incarnations of self and other. This phrase recalls the image in the first section of the text, of the two streams of the river flowing together again, and in a sense 'recuperates' it as an image of the protagonist's relationship with the lost other, as well as confirming the growing intimacy between the two identical figures on stage, already established through the gestures. The linearity of the narrative is transformed into the 'dream' space common to text and stage, in which self and other meet and merge, though without (yet) surrendering difference.

From this point on, the text moves towards closure. In the narrative, after the last reading has ended, the two figures remain quite still, their bodies petrified, while the 'self' has passed beyond form and even being, beyond all dualities and dichotomies, to the ultimate comfort evoked in one of Beckett's poems entitled 'Neither':

> till at last halt for good, absent for good
> from self and other
>
> then no sound
>
> then gently light unfading on that unheeded
> neither
>
> unspeakable home

The closure of the text on silence and stillness is emphasized by the final phrase, 'Nothing is left to tell'. This closure is not reflected on stage, however. After the book has been closed, the two figures do not remain immobile, but slowly lower their hands from their brows and raise their heads to meet each other's gaze. This gesture thus contradicts the closure of the narrative, and tends to emphasize the persistence of consciousness, rather than unconsciousness. On the other hand, we are aware that the end is imminent and the final moments therefore also anticipate that final closure (of performance, play, being and telling) after the last even of last tales has been told. The various times evoked during the performance merge into the 'here and now' of the stage present, poised on the blink of oblivion:

> by a typically Beckettian focus, the 'nothing left' results not simply from present and future merging (and thus no more time) but rather from past and present merging and thus no more memory, that is no more consciousness, and thus, of course, no more time.[41]

As the light narrows in to focus on the two profiles, the different spaces and identities also merge, metamorphose and finally condense themselves into this single, dual image, held for ten seconds before final fade-out: a concentrated image of the essential schism within the self, but also a visual realization of the moment of intimacy and communion longed for but never achieved in *Rockaby*. The divisions between the self-creating and the self-created, between a life and the story of that life, are reconciled. As in *Rockaby*, the process of reconciliation is linked to the ritual of narration, which creates a 'privileged space' in which fixed boundaries merge and metamorphose one into the other. In *Ohio Impromptu*, this merging also challenges notions of the authority and origins of fiction.

While the scenic level suggests that the Listener is both author and subject of the tale being read, the text presents the provenance of the 'sad tale' as entirely 'other': as originating from an other being/non-being and an other place or space where the very distinction between being and non-being, absence and presence, origin and end seems meaningless. The 'shade' of the narrative crosses the boundaries between life and death and between identities (it is associated yet not identified with the 'dear face' and becomes 'as one' with the protagonist). Indeed, *Ohio Impromptu* seems to be founded on a dual desire: the desire for an 'other' to relieve the isolation or 'lack' of being and the desire to be done with selves and others, in the still, silent world beyond time and space. The play, however, presents a shade of comfort in the form of the fiction. The tale/telling provides the self with a story and an other (self) for company. Like the traditional Japanese ritual described by Yasunari Takahashi, which centres on 'the preparation of a sacred space, a kind of purified "void", so that the empty space might be filled by the arrival of a strange guest, a sacred spirit in human form',[42] it also creates a space in which a dialogue between self and other, being and non-being, can be established, providing a refuge from self-hood, until such comfort is no longer necessary. The fiction, indeed, creates a no-man's-land between life and death, where the telling of the tale performs the rites of passage.

Ohio Impromptu therefore draws attention to a paradox which recurs through Beckett's work. On the one hand, there is a valorization of the 'ideal absence' which affirms the transcendental bias of Western epistemology, manifest in the yearning of Beckett's characters to be gone. On the other, the creative impulse and process, even when it anticipates or rehearses that annihilation, also defies and defers it, creating a medium in which absence and presence, form and space, self and other are not oppositional, but through an alchemy of dramatic ritual and discipline, continually correspond and metamorphose, one into the other.

CONCLUSION: BECKETT AND PERFORMANCE – BACK TO THE FUTURE

Part of Beckett's importance as a cultural figure is that he blurs ordinary distinctions between mainstream and avant-garde. Because he was embraced so readily as a classic he was able, in effect, to smuggle ideas across the border of mainstream culture, and that achievement is, rightfully, his most celebrated: he has actually changed many people's expectations about what can happen, what is supposed to happen, when they enter a theatre. Not surprisingly, then, many avant-gardists . . . perceive this achievement as already ancient history and assume that their own work represents a radical departure from Beckett's. Actually, though, his work, particularly the media and late plays, remains in certain ways just as radical, as unassimilable into traditional structures of theatrical production, as theirs.[1]

The persisting humanism in Beckett is not mere tokenism of balancing forces – some from the old world some from the new – it is a single world moving and being moved in an almost classical structure of incoherence through interminable division. Nothing Disappears.[2]

Both Herbert Blau and Jonathan Kalb situate Beckett as belonging to an aesthetic which is both anterior to contemporary performance[3] and yet, in some ways, opens up areas which contemporary theatrical practitioners are only beginning to fully explore. While Beckett remains largely within a Modernist context, framed by a white, Western male epistemology, he is also attacking some of its central tenets. Indeed, I believe Beckett's continuing significance lies in the weight of literary and philosophical heritage which even his most minimal plays evoke. Beckett's work presents a sustained

123

critique of this heritage and the extent to which it infiltrates even the most intimate areas of our experience, revealing the construction of identity to be linked to dominant forms of representation and knowledge. Beckett's later plays both parody the repressive mechanisms of logocentric representation and trace an alternative representational practice. They enact a continual, imaginative process of transformation and metamorphosis in which forms are not only dissociated from their meanings but form new syntheses, where the boundaries between the inner and the outer worlds, between the visible and the invisible, are eroded.

Indeed, if a number of theories have been 'synthesized' in this study it is in the belief that Beckett has condensed many levels and layers of meaning and references into these works, which constitute also a conscious rereading of the texts of the past and of the representative practices of the past, the complexity of which is only beginning to be discovered in the light of current philosophy's or critical theory's rereading of the texts which have formed our conceptual and aesthetic heritage: from the writings of the classics to the philosophical and literary texts of the nineteenth and early twentieth century. The theoretical texts that I have most relied on – Derrida, Lacan, Kristeva and Irigaray – also constitute a return to and rereading of previous texts and discourses. Such a process of synthesis and such a wide range of discourses cannot, of course, be adequately 'contained' or mastered by this study, which aims rather to suggest a series of contexts which may illuminate Beckett's dramatic practice in these later plays.

I have therefore tried to 'ground' the study in a concrete analysis of Beckett's theatrical practice and on detailed analyses of individual plays in order to counter the breadth of focus evoked by the multiple theoretical frameworks. This practice was also based on an approach which sees Beckett's engagement with the philosophical frameworks of the past as firmly rooted in his engagement with the materials of whatever medium he is working in. Beckett's theatre therefore offers a rigorous interrogation of the languages and strategies of theatrical presentation and signification. Beckett's questioning of the fundamental codes of the theatre, inevitably problematizes the audience–stage relationship. While apparently placing the audience in a voyeuristic role, Beckett both frames and subverts the role of the audience as consumer. Since the fragmented structure of the plays creates a dynamic interplay of meaning within and between text and stage, or indeed, frequently deflects or deflates meaning, and since the processes of perception and signification are foregrounded in performance, the audience is forced to actively participate in the construction or 'deconstruction' of signification.

This interruption of the processes of signification in the theatre raises issues around theories of reading theatre. A number of recent critics have questioned the dominance of theatre semiotics as the most fruitful method of analysing theatre. Semiotics was extremely useful in establishing the specificity of theatre and in the articulation of a vocabulary with which to analyse theatre performance. However, as Maria Minich Brewer suggests, traditional theatre semiology presents a rather unproblematic view of the processes of signification and interpretation:

> What happens to semiotic oppositions when they are challenged by the most diverse of theatrical practices? The question of theatricality can no longer simply be viewed from within a formal, intrinsic understanding of the sign, for each element of the general opposition between signifier and signified, frame and content, inside and outside, is questioned by practices that displace any notion of theatricality as closure. Formal frames give way to contextual ones, or rather formal frames are increasingly being thought of as contextually motivated and determined. The undoing of the limits of representation involves a shift in the understanding of theatricality, a shift Lyotard has described as the tendency toward desemiotization in the theatre.[4]

Beckett's strategic interruption of the processes of signification and interpretation, his foregrounding of the body as both framed in representation and yet also resisting those frames,[5] his ruthless investigation of processes of perception and his interest in technology are at the forefront of contemporary theoretical and performance issues. Beckett's significance may lie in his very position on the borderline between mastery and resistance, between the ruins of the past and the possibility of new discourses and representational practices.

NOTES

INTRODUCTION

1 Josette Féral, 'Performance and Theatricality', trans. Teresa Lyons, *Modern Drama*, XXV, 1, 1982, p. 178.
2 Elinor Fuchs, 'Presence and the Revenge of Writing: Rethinking Theatre After Derrida', *Performing Arts Journal*, 26/27, 1985, p. 172.
3 Roland Barthes, *On Racine*, trans. Richard Howard, New York, Performing Arts Journal Publications, 1983, p. viii.
4 David Watson, *Paradox and Desire in Beckett's Fiction*, London, Macmillan, 1991, p. 83.
5 ibid. p. 82.
6 Jacques Derrida, *Writing and Difference*, trans. Alan Bass, London, Routledge, 1978, pp. 279–80.
7 See Hélène Cixous on 'death-dealing' patriarchal binary thought in 'Sorties', *The Newly Born Woman*, with Catherine Clement, trans. Betsy Wing, Manchester, Manchester University Press, 1986.
8 Jacques Derrida, *Dissemination*, trans. Barbara Johnson, London, Athlone Press, 1981, p. 193.
9 Quoted in Keir Elam, *The Semiotics of Theatre and Drama*, London, Methuen, 1980, p. 113.
10 Elinor Fuchs, op. cit. p. 163.
11 Elin Diamond, 'Mimesis, Mimicry and the True-Real', *Modern Drama*, XXXII, 1, 1989, p. 62.
12 Jacques Derrida, *Writing and Difference*, p. 280.
13 Maria Minich Brewer, 'Performing Theory', *Theatre Journal*, 37, 1985, p. 16.
14 Samuel Beckett, *Not I*, in *Collected Shorter Plays*, London, Faber, 1986, p. 221. All references to Beckett's later drama will be to this edition. Within each chapter, page references to the *Collected Shorter Plays* will be given in parentheses after the quotation.
15 Lacan assumes that the Symbolic only recognizes masculine subjects and that the woman has no place in the signifying system – therefore she cannot speak or know herself. Feminist critics have pointed out Lacan's endorsement of the exclusion of women from the Symbolic reflected in his use of the masculine pronoun as the universal subject.

Where this occurs in Lacan's or other texts, I have bracketed the term.

16 Jacques Lacan, *Ecrits: A Selection*, trans. Alan Sheridan, London, Tavistock, 1977, p. 2.

17 ibid. p. 106.

18 ibid. p. 67. Judith Butler has noted the danger of adopting a 'transcultural notion of patriarchy' which does not take into account cultural differences, in *Gender Trouble*, London, Routledge, 1990, p. 35. Yet the laws of patriarchy promote this universalizing tendency. Lacan's cultural frame of reference is largely Western, white and male. As such, however, his theories provide a useful starting point for a critique and possible subversion of the ways in which these values permeate the signifying systems of Western societies and those societies colonized by the West.

19 Jacques Lacan, op. cit. p. 86.

20 ibid. p. 103.

21 ibid. p. 104.

22 Julia Kristeva, *Revolution in Poetic Language*, trans. Margaret Waller, New York, Columbia University Press, 1984, pp. 25–6.

23 ibid. p. 35.

24 Jacques Derrida, 'The Theatre of Cruelty and the Closure of Representation', in *Writing and Difference*, p. 235.

25 Keir Elam, op. cit. p. 99.

26 Josette Féral, op. cit. pp. 177–8.

27 See Alice Jardine, *Gynesis: Configurations of Woman and Modernity*, Ithaca, NY, Cornell University Press, 1985, p. 71: 'the crisis in the discursive itineraries of Western philosophy and the human sciences isomorphic to it involves first and foremost a problematization of the boundaries and spaces necessary to their existence.'

28 Steven Connor, *Samuel Beckett: Repetition, Theory and Text*, Oxford, Blackwell, 1988, p. 124.

29 Joseph Melançon, 'Theatre as Semiotic Practice', *Modern Drama*, XXV, 1, 1982, pp. 21–2.

30 ibid. p. 17.

31 ibid. p. 18.

32 Michel Foucault, *Discipline and Punish: The Birth of the Prison*, trans. Alan Sheridan, London, Penguin, 1977, p.25.

33 Rosi Braidotti, 'The Politics of Ontological Difference', in *Between Feminism and Psychoanalysis*, ed. Teresa Brennan, London, Routledge, 1989, p. 97.

34 Stanton B. Garner, 'Visual Field in Beckett's Late Plays', *Comparative Drama*, XXI, 4, 1987–8, p. 356.

35 Rosi Braidotti, *Patterns of Dissonance*, Cambridge, Polity Press, 1991, p. 10.

1 MIMICKING MIMESIS

1 Elin Diamond, 'Mimesis, Mimicry and the "True-Real" ', *Modern Drama*, XXXII, 1, 1989, p. 65.

2 Herbert Blau, *Take Up The Bodies: Theatre At The Vanishing Point*, Urbana, IL, University of Illinois Press, 1982, p. 25.

3 Jurgen Habermas, in *The Anti-Aesthetic: Essays on Postmodern Culture*, ed. Hal Foster, Port Townsend, Bay Press, 1985, p. 9.

4 David Harvey, *The Condition of Postmodernity*, Oxford, Blackwell, 1989, p. 13.

5 Michel Foucault, *Discipline and Punish: The Birth of the Prison*, trans. Alan Sheridan, Harmondsworth, Penguin, 1977, p. 170.

6 Samuel Beckett, *Play*, in *Collected Shorter Plays*, p. 156.

7 Jane Gallop, *Reading Lacan*, Ithaca, NY, Cornell University Press, 1985, pp. 79, 81.

8 Jacques Lacan, *Ecrits: A Selection*, trans. Alan Sheridan, London, Tavistock, 1977, p. 2.

9 ibid. pp. 2–3.

10 Jane Gallop, op. cit. p. 80.

11 Jacques Lacan, 'Some Reflections on the Ego', *International Journal of Psychoanalysis*, 34, 1953, p. 15.

12 W. B. Worthen, 'Playing *Play*', *Theatre Journal*, December 1985, p. 406.

13 See Martin Esslin, 'Samuel Beckett and the Art of Broadcasting', *Encounter*, September 1975.

14 ibid. p. 44: 'The text fell into three parts: Chorus (all the characters speaking simultaneously), Narration (in which the characters talk about the events which led to the catastrophe), and Meditation (in which they reflect on their state of being endlessly suspended in limbo).'

15 Jacques Derrida, 'LIVING ON: *Border Lines*', in *Deconstruction and Criticism*, ed. Harold Bloom *et al.*, London, Routledge & Kegan Paul, 1979, pp. 104–5.

16 I am using the Structuralist distinction between *story* and *discourse*, or that of the Russian Formalists, between *fabula* and *plot*, as outlined by Seymour Chatman in *Story and Discourse: Narrative Structure in Fiction and Film*, Ithaca, NY, Cornell University Press, 1978, p. 19 ff. *Story* or *fabula* refers to 'the sum total of events to be related in the narrative', while the *discourse* or *plot* constitutes 'the story as actually told by linking the events together'.

17 See Paul Lawley, 'Beckett's dramatic counterpoint: a reading of *Play*', *Journal of Beckett Studies*, 9, pp. 35–6.

18 Andrew Kennedy, *Six Dramatists in Search of a Language*, Cambridge, Cambridge University Press, 1975, pp. 137–9.

19 George Devine, manuscript notes for the first production of *Play* in England, presented at the Old Vic, London, March 1964. RUL MS 1581/15.

20 ibid.

21 Lacan himself described such a process under the term of *aphanisis*: 'when the subject appears somewhere as meaning, he is manifested elsewhere as 'fading', as disappearance.' *The Four Fundamental Concepts of Psychoanalysis*, trans. Alan Sheridan, Harmondsworth, Penguin, 1977, p. 218.

22 W.B. Worthen, op. cit. pp. 408, 412.

23 Michel Foucault, op. cit. p. 143.
24 ibid. pp. 170–1.
25 Peter Gidal, *Understanding Beckett*, London, Macmillan, 1986, p. 39.
26 Philip Monk, 'Common Carrier: Performance by Artists', *Modern Drama*, XXV, 1, p. 167.
27 Michel Foucault, op. cit. p. 185.
28 Bert O. States, '*Catastrophe*: Beckett's Laboratory/Theatre', *Modern Drama*, XXX, 1, 1987, p. 15.
29 Michel Foucault, op. cit. pp. 137–8.
30 H. Porter Abbott, 'Tyranny and Theatricality', *Theatre Journal*, 1988, p. 87.
31 Frank Lazarus, 'One in the Mouth', *The Guardian*, Tuesday 24 November 1987.
32 Barbara Freedman, 'Frame-up: Feminism, Psychoanalysis, Theatre' in *Performing Feminisms: Feminist Critical Theory and Theatre*, ed. Sue-Ellen Case, Baltimore, MD, Johns Hopkins University Press, 1990, p. 74.
33 Herbert Blau, op. cit. p. 21.
34 Martha Fehsenfeld, ' "Everything out but the Faces": Beckett's Re-shaping of *What Where* for Television', *Modern Drama*, XXIX, 1986, p. 240.
35 Quoted in translation in Steven Connor, *Samuel Beckett: Repetition, Theory and Text*, Oxford, Blackwell, 1988, pp. 7–8.
36 Samuel Taylor Coleridge, *Biographia Literaria*, London: J.M. Dent, 1906, p. 159.
37 Edward Casey, 'Imagination and Repetition in Literature: A Reassessment', *Yale French Studies*, 52, 1975, pp. 254–5.
38 ibid. p. 259.
39 ibid. p. 255.
40 ibid. p. 263.
41 Steven Connor, *Samuel Beckett: Repetition, Theory and Text*, Oxford, Blackwell, 1988, p 130.
42 Samuel Beckett, notebook for the television version of *Was Wo*, RUL MS 3097.
43 ibid.
44 Jacques Derrida, 'The Double Session', in *Dissemination*, trans. Barbara Johnson, London, Athlone Press, 1981, p. 234.
45 See Martha Fehsenfeld, op. cit. p. 236.
46 ibid. p. 237.
47 ibid. p. 238.
48 From the text of *Mimique* quoted in Jacques Derrida, op. cit. p. 175.
49 Friedrich Nietzsche, *The Will to Power*, ed. Walter Kaufmann, New York, Vintage Books, 1986, p. 547.
50 Jacques Derrida, op. cit. p. 187.
51 Friedrich Nietzsche, *The Dawn of Day*, New York, Gordon Press, 1974, p. 45.
52 Samuel Beckett, *Rough for Radio II*, Collected Shorter Plays of Samuel Beckett, London, Faber, 1984, p.121.
53 ibid. p. 122.
54 Peter Gidal, op. cit. p. 242.

55 Martha Fehsenfeld, op. cit. p. 237.
56 Jacques Derrida, 'The Double Session', p. 208.

2 MASQUERADES OF SELF

1 Michel Foucault, 'Nietzsche, Genealogy, History', in *The Foucault Reader*, ed. Paul Rabinow, Harmondsworth, Penguin, 1986, p. 94.
2 Samuel Beckett, *That Time*, in *Collected Shorter Plays*, p. 230.
3 Barbara Freedman, *Staging the Gaze: Postmodernism, Psychoanalysis and Shakespearean Comedy*, Ithaca, NY, Cornell University Press, 1991, p. 52.
4 Juliet Flower MacCannell, *The Regime of the Brother*, London, Routledge, 1991, p. 44.
5 ibid. p. 34.
6 Barbara Freedman's article considers the implications of the model of the maternal gaze for a reassessment of the position of the spectator in the theatre. Whereas the maternal function in Lacanian theory simply reinforces the paternal law, Freedman sees the maternal gaze as one which challenges and deflects the assumption of identity and power. In general, many feminist theorists are concerned, not with the wholesale rejection of identity and authority, but with the possibility of reconstructing and redeploying identity and authority in non-repressive forms. The maternal function is often central to this project. See works by Luce Irigaray, Julia Kristeva and Hélène Cixous.
7 Michel Foucault, op. cit. p. 78.
8 James Knowlson, in *Frescoes of the Skull*, James Knowlson and John Pilling (eds), London, Calder, 1979, p. 219.
9 Stanton B. Garner, 'Visual Field in Beckett's Late Plays', *Comparative Drama*, XXI, 4, 1987–8, p. 371.
10 This was particularly true of the production at the Théâtre Gérard Philippe, St-Denis, Paris, in 1983, when David Warrilow played the role of the Souvenant. The audience occupied the balcony while the stalls were completely empty, so that the stage space merged with the space of the lower auditorium and the spotlit image viewed from above seemed to appear in the midst of an immense, dark void.
11 Samuel Beckett, *Proust and Three Dialogues*, London, Calder, 1965, p. 58.
12 ibid. pp. 17–18.
13 Walter Asmus, 'Rehearsal notes for the German première of *That Time* and *Footfalls* at the Schiller-Theater Werkstatt, Berlin', *Journal of Beckett Studies*, 2, 1977, p. 92.
14 Gérard Genette, *Figures of Literary Discourse*, trans. Alan Sheridan, Oxford, Blackwell, 1982, p. 136.
15 ibid. p. 138.
16 Mikhail Bakhtin, *The Dialogic Imagination*, ed. Michael Holquist, trans. Caryl Emerson and Michael Holquist, Austin, TX, University of Texas Press, 1981, p. 84.
17 ibid. p. 132.
18 ibid. p. 135–6.
19 Quoted by John Pilling in *Frescoes of the Skull*, Knowlson and Pilling, p. 135.

20 Mikhail Bakhtin, *The Dialogic Imagination*, p. 120.

21 James Knowlson, in *Frescoes of the Skull*, Knowlson and Pilling, p. 216.

22 Samuel Beckett, 'The Vulture', *Collected Poems 1930–1978*, London, Calder, 1986, p. 9.

23 S. E. Gontarski, *The Intent of Undoing in Samuel Beckett's Dramatic Texts*, Bloomington, IN, Indiana University Press, 1985, p. 173.

24 See Linda · Ben-Zvi, 'The Schismatic Self in *A Piece of Monologue*', *Journal of Beckett Studies*, 7, 1982. p. 15: 'The play ends on the growing pull of the image of death.'

25 When David Warrilow played the Récitant in the production of *Solo* which accompanied the afore-mentioned performance of *Cette fois* at the Théâtre Gérard Philippe in Paris, in 1983, there were some slight movements, but these are not indicated in the text.

26 The television plays *Ghost Trio* and *. . . but the clouds . . .* , as well as the stage play *Footfalls* (1975), were written between *That Time* (1974) and *A Piece of Monologue* (1977).

27 'Eye ravening patient in the haggard vulture face, perhaps its carrion time', *Texts for Nothing I*, in *Collected Shorter Prose*, London, Calder, 1984, p. 73. The 'ravening eye' is frequently mentioned in the later prose works and is of central importance in *Ill seen Ill Said*.

28 *. . . but the clouds . . .* , *Collected Shorter Plays of Samuel Beckett*, London, Faber, 1984, p. 259.

29 Linda Ben-Zvi, op. cit. p 11.

30 S.E. Gontarski, op. cit. p. 173.

31 I have generally referred to the stage figure as 'the speaker' and the figure in the narrative as 'the protagonist'.

32 'Still', in *Collected Shorter Prose 1945–1980*, London, Calder, p. 183.

33 See the prose text, *Lessness*, for a more extreme example of this process, discussed in Martin Esslin's article, 'Samuel Beckett – Infinity, Eternity', in *Beckett at 80: Beckett in Context*, ed. Brater, pp. 110–23.

34 There is perhaps a parallel to be made with the end of Eugène Ionesco's *Le Roi se Meurt*, where the death of the individual/king corresponds with the dissolution of his kingdom.

35 This is another example of Beckett denying the audience's presence while drawing attention to the theatrical illusion from which his stage world is constructed.

36 Samuel Beckett, *Company*, London, Calder, 1980, p. 64.

37 For a discussion of Beckett's use of the pastoral, see Stephen Watt, 'Beckett by Way of Baudrillard: Toward a Political Reading of Samuel Beckett's Drama', in *Myth and Ritual in the Plays of Samuel Beckett*, ed. Katherine H. Burkman, New Jersey, Associated University Presses, 1987, pp. 103–23.

38 Rosi Braidotti, *Patterns of Dissonance*, Cambridge, Polity Press, 1991, p. 24.

39 *Modern Drama*, XXV, 1, 1982, pp. 349–54.

40 Rosi Braidotti, op. cit. p. 10.

3 THIS SEX WHICH IS NOT ONE

1 Judith Butler, *Gender Trouble*, London, Routledge, 1990, p. 9.
2 Luce Irigaray, *The Irigaray Reader*, ed. Margaret Whitford, Oxford, Blackwell, 1991, p. 59.
3 Rosi Braidotti, *Patterns of Dissonance*, Cambridge, Polity Press, 1991, p. 11.
4 Judith Butler, op. cit. p. 56.
5 Luce Irigaray, *This Sex Which Is Not One*, trans. Catherine Porter, Ithaca, NY, Cornell University Press, 1985, p. 30.
6 Rosi Braidotti, op. cit. p. 133.
7 Linda Ben-Zvi, ed., *Women in Beckett: Performance and Critical Perspectives*, Urbana, IL, University of Illinois Press, 1990.
8 Linda Ben-Zvi notes that it is in these stage dramas that 'women emerge as full-drawn, independent figures in their own right'. ibid. p. xii.
9 See, for example, articles by Dina Sherzer, 'The Experience of Marginality in *Not I*', and Ann Wilson, 'The Castrated Voice of *Not I*', in *Women in Beckett*, ed. Linda Ben-Zvi. The charge of voyeurism is most frequently applied to the television version of the play, see Linda Ben-Zvi's article in *Women in Beckett*.
10 Paul Lawley, 'Counterpoint, Absence and the Medium in Beckett's *Not I*', *Modern Drama*, XXVI, 4, 1983, p. 412.
11 Jacques Lacan, 'Subversion of the Subject and Dialectic of Desire', in *Ecrits: A Selection*, trans. Alan Sheridan, London, Tavistock, 1977, pp. 314–15.
12 Although, according to film theory, voyeurism is usually related to the fetishization of the female body or bodily parts as an attempt to mask the threat of castration which the woman represents for the male. See Laura Mulvey, 'Visual Pleasure and Narrative Cinema' *Screen*, 16, 3, 1975, pp. 6–180.
13 See Anika Lemaire, *Jacques Lacan*, trans. David Maloy, London, Routledge & Kegan Paul, 1977, p. 57: 'The first of the distinctions effected by the symbolic register of language – the distinction between interior and exterior – is particularly vital for the "subject".' See also Frederick Jamieson, *Yale French Studies*, 1977, No. 55–6, p. 356: 'there is . . . a logic specific to Imaginary space, whose dominant category proves to be the opposition of container and contained, the fundamental relationship of inside to outside, which clearly enough originates in the infant's fantasies about the maternal body as receptacle of part-objects (confusion between childbirth and evacuation, etc.).'
14 Luce Irigaray, *This Sex Which Is Not One*, op. cit. p. 117.
15 ibid. p. 26.
16 See 'Not I – synopsis', typescript by Samuel Beckett, RUL MS 1227/7/12/10.
17 Paul Lawley, op. cit. p. 409.
18 ibid. p. 411.
19 ibid. p. 409.

20 Elizabeth Wright, *Psychoanalytic Criticism: Theory in Practice*, London, Methuen, 1984, p. 113.

21 The concept of 'desiring production' in the work of Gilles Deleuze and Felix Guatarri is relevant here. See *Anti-Oedipus: Capitalism and Schizophrenia*, trans. Robert Hurley, Mark Seem and Helen Riane, Minneapolis, MN, University of Minnesota Press, 1983.

22 Keir Elam, in *Beckett at 80: Beckett in Context*, ed. Enoch Brater, New York, Oxford University Press, 1986, p. 146.

23 Julia Kristeva, *Desire in Language: A Semiotic Approach to Literature and Art*, Oxford, Blackwell, 1980, pp. 148–58.

24 While the Auditor is described as being of 'indeterminate sex', critics have almost always referred to the figure as 'he'. This may be due to the fact that the figure seems to include judgement as well as sympathy or perhaps because the figure seems to represent the specular form, however veiled, which Mouth lacks. However, neither the scenic nor the verbal text definitively assign a specific gender position to the Auditor. I have used brackets around the masculine pronoun when designating the Auditor to indicate gender ambiguity. This ambiguity reflects the Auditor's ambiguous relation to Mouth. While [he] may be an external observer, [he] may be a projected aspect of Mouth's fragmented psyche. Instead of a single opposition between self and other, the play presents a complex series of oppositions between selves and others.

25 Keir Elam, op. cit. p. 143.

26 Jacques Lacan, *The Four Fundamental Concepts of Psychoanalysis*, Harmondsworth, Penguin, 1979, p. 92.

27 See the article by Josette Féral quoted in the introduction, *Modern Drama*, XXV, 1, 1982, p. 171.

28 ibid. p. 179.

29 Chantal Pontbriand, 'The Eye Finds no Fixed Point on Which to Rest', *Modern Drama*, XXV, 1, 1982, p. 156.

30 Paul Newham, 'The Voice and the Shadow', *Performance*, 60, 1990, p. 44.

31 Helga Finter, 'Experimental Theatre and Semiology of Theatre: The Theatricalisation of Voice', *Modern Drama*, XXVI, 4, 1983, p. 512.

32 Although *Breath* falls within the chronological scope of the later plays, I felt that the absence of textual/scenic interaction – since there is no text as such – justified its exclusion from the present study.

33 RUL MS 1227/7/16/4–5. One of these drafts is entitled 'Good Heavens' and is inscribed by Beckett 'Before Come and Go'.

34 Rosemary Pountney, *Theatre of Shadows: Samuel Beckett's Drama 1956–76*, Irish Literary Studies, Gerrards Cross, Colin Smythe, 1988, p. 78. A detailed study of the evolution of the play is given in pages 76–86.

35 ibid. p. 78.

36 James Knowlson, in *Frescoes of the Skull*, James Knowlson and John Pilling (eds), London, Calder, 1979, p. 124.

37 Hersch Zeifman, *'Come and Go: A Criticule'*, in *Samuel Beckett: Humanistic Perspectives*, ed. Morris Beja, S.E. Gontarski and Pierre Astier, Columbus, OH, Ohio State University Press, 1983, p. 142.

38 In his extremely useful study, *Beckett in Performance*, Cambridge, Cambridge University Press, 1989, Jonathan Kalb contrasts acting techniques in the early and the later drama, confirming Beckett's increasing departure in the later plays from traditional notions of character.

39 Paul Newham, op. cit. p. 45.

40 Rosemary Pountney, op. cit. p. 85.

41 RUL MS 1227/7/16/4.

42 ibid. p. 121.

43 Rosemary Pountney argues that this may be the original version, but she is not entirely convincing.

44 Hersch Zeifman, op. cit. p 139.

45 ibid. p. 142.

46 Knowlson and Pilling, (eds), *Frescoes of the Skull*, p. 123.

47 Ruby Cohn, *Just Play: Beckett's Theatre*, Princeton, NJ, Princeton University Press, 1980, p. 235.

48 Hersch Zeifman, op. cit. p. 142.

49 Stanton Garner, 'Visual Field in Beckett's Late Plays', *Comparative Drama*, XXI, 4, 1987–8, p. 357.

4 REFIGURING AUTHORITY

1 Judith Butler, *Gender Trouble*, London, Routledge, 1990, p. 57.

2 Jacques Lacan, *Ecrits: A Selection*, trans. Alan Sheridan, London, Tavistock, 1977, p. 105.

3 See Serge Lebovici and Daniel Widlocher, eds, *Psychoanalysis in France*, New York, International University Press, 1980.

4 Judith Butler, op. cit. p. 68.

5 In 'Melancholia and Mourning' and 'The Ego and the Id', *The Penguin Freud Library*, Vol. 11, *On Metapsychology: The Theory of Psychoanalysis*, Harmondsworth, Penguin, 1984, Freud argues that the loss of a desired object can cause the libido to transfer onto the ego itself. Juliet Flower MacCannell's *The Regime of the Brother*, London, Routledge, 1991, analyses this inability to recognize difference, which she sees as founded on a denial of the role of the woman, in relation to forms of narrative in selected philosophical and literary texts.

6 See 'Women–mothers, the silent substratum', in *The Irigaray Reader*, ed. Margaret Whitford, Oxford, Blackwell, 1991. By contrast, many myths and narratives figure the struggle between fathers and sons.

7 Jessica Benjamin, in *Between Feminism and Psychoanalysis*, ed. Teresa Brennan, London, Routledge, 1989 p. 134.

8 This could be seen in the light of MacCannell's arguments as an erasure of the woman, leaving the subject face to face with his fraternal alter-ego. However, in the regime of the brother, need itself is denied, and this need or desire which crosses gender boundaries is the animating force of Beckett's work.

9 See Walter Asmus, 'Rehearsal Notes for the German Première of Beckett's *That Time*, and *Footfalls* at the Schiller Theater Werkstatt, Berlin', *Journal of Beckett Studies*, 2, Summer 1977, pp. 83–4, which reports Beckett's account of this lecture during rehearsals, and also

the text of *All That Fall*, London, Faber and Faber, 1957, pp. 33–4: '[The doctor – "one of those new mind doctors"] could find nothing wrong with her, he said . . . the trouble with her was that she had never really been born.'

10 ibid. pp. 83–5.

11 S. E. Gontarski, *The Intent of Undoing*, Bloomington, IN, Indiana University Press, 1985, pp. 244–5.

12 Keir Elam, '*Not I*: Beckett's Mouth and the Ars(e) Rhetorica', in *Beckett at 80: Beckett in Context*, ed. Brater, New York, Oxford University Press, 1986, p. 140.

13 Walter Asmus, op. cit. p. 85.

14 Julia Kristeva, 'The Ruin of a Poetics', in *Russian Formalism*, ed. Stephen Bann and John E. Bowlt, Edinburgh, Scottish Academic Press, 1973, p. 109.

15 In the second manuscript Beckett included the line 'My voice is in her head', although subsequently erased it, RUL 1552/2.

16 Walter Asmus, op. cit. p. 86.

17 Peter Gidal, *Understanding Beckett*, London, Macmillan, 1986, p. 163.

18 In Roland Barthes, *Image–Music–Text*, London, Fontana, 1977, p. 69.

19 James Knowlson and John Pilling (eds), *Frescoes of the Skull*, London, Calder, p. 226.

20 Peter Gidal, op. cit. p. 162.

21 Julia Kristeva, *Revolution in Poetic Language*, New York, Columbia University Press, 1984, p. 241.

22 Jane Hale, *The Broken Window: Beckett's Dramatic Perspective*, Indiana, Purdue University Press, 1987, p. 138.

23 Hersch Zeifman, ' "The Core of the Eddy": *Rockaby* and Dramatic Genre', in *Beckett Translating: Translating Beckett*, eds Alan Friedman, Charles Rossman and Dina Sherzer, University Park, PA, Pennsylvania University Press, 1987, p. 141.

24 Carol Cook, 'Unbodied Figures of Desire', *Theatre Journal*, March 1986, p 46.

25 'The woman in no way initiates the rock', quoted from Beckett (to Danny Labeille) by Enoch Brater in *Beyond Minimalism*, New York, Oxford University Press, 1987, p. 173.

26 Charles Lyons, 'Perceiving *Rockaby*: As a text, as a Text by Samuel Beckett, as a Text for Performance', *Comparative Drama*, Vol. 16, No. 4, Winter 1982–3, p. 307.

27 Enoch Brater, op. cit. p. 168.

28 ibid. p. 168.

29 Charles Lyons, op. cit. p. 307.

30 Samuel Beckett, *Collected Shorter Plays*, London, Faber, 1986, p. 280.

31 Hersch Zeifman, op. cit. p. 145.

32 ibid. pp. 144, 146.

33 See Jane Hale, op. cit. p. 144: 'Beckett is dramatizing a problem that has long intrigued him: the temporal gap that must occur at the moment of death between the perceiving consciousness and its object, the perceived self.'

34 Pierre Astier, 'Beckett's *Ohio Impromptu*: A View from the Isle of Swans', *Modern Drama*, XXV, 3, 1982, p. 332.

35 ibid. p. 338.

36 Kristin Morrison has argued that the narrative in Beckett's plays both presents and displaces such emotions, revealing 'deep and difficult thoughts and feelings while at the same time concealing or at least distancing them as narration', *Canters and Chronicles: The Use of Narrative in the Plays of Samuel Beckett and Harold Pinter*, Chicago, Il, University of Chicago Press, 1983, p. 3.

37 Suzanne Langer, *Feeling and Form*, London, Routledge & Kegan Paul, 1953, p. 52.

38 Title of previously quoted article by Linda Ben-Zvi, *Journal of Beckett Studies*, 7, 1982, pp. 7–17.

39 Linda Anderson, 'At the Threshold of the Self: Women and Autobiography', in *Women's Writing: A Challenge to Theory*, ed. Moira Monteith, Brighton, Harvester Press, 1986, p. 59.

40

> ESTRAGON: Perhaps the other is called Cain. Cain! Cain!
> POZZO: Help!
> ESTRAGON: He's all humanity.

Samuel Beckett, *Waiting For Godot*, London, Faber and Faber, 1956, p. 83.

41 Kristin Morrison, op. cit. p. 122.

42 Yasunari Takahashi, 'The Theatre of Mind: Samuel Beckett and the Noh', *Encounter*, LVIII, 4, 1982, p. 66.

CONCLUSION

1 Jonathan Kalb, *Beckett in Performance*, Cambridge, Cambridge University Press, 1989, pp. 157–8.

2 Herbert Blau, 'Take Up the Bodies', *Theatre at the Vanishing Point*, Urbana, IL, University of Illinois Press, 1982, p. 21.

3 I am referring both to contemporary theatre and to performance art, which crosses the genres of dance, media, art and theatre. There is a mutual influence, particularly in the work of American experimental practitioners like Richard Foreman or the Wooster Group.

4 Maria Minich Brewer, 'Performing Theory', *Theatre Journal*, 37, 1, 1985, p. 19.

5 See Elin Diamond 'Mimesis, Mimicry and the "True-Real" ', *Modern Drama*, XXXII, 1, 1989, pp. 58–72; Susan Foster, 'The Signifying Body: Reaction and Resistance in Postmodern Dance', *Theatre Journal*, 37, 1, 1985, pp. 45–64; or Wladimir Krysinski, 'Semiotic modalities of the Body in Modern Drama', *Poetics Today*, 2, 3, Spring 1981, pp. 141–61.

BIBLIOGRAPHY

MANUSCRIPTS OF SAMUEL BECKETT AND RELATED MANUSCRIPTS CONSULTED

The manuscripts are listed alphabetically by play title, given in the language of original composition. The date of completion of the original version is given in brackets after the title and is based on Ruby Cohn's compilation, aided by James Knowlson, in the *Casebook on Waiting for Godot*, ed. Ruby Cohn. The MS numbers refer to the collection in the University of Reading Library. The descriptions follow for the most part the descriptions given in *The Samuel Beckett Collection: a Catalogue*, The Library, University of Reading, 1978, and in subsequent supplements.

A Piece of Monologue (originally entitled *Gone*) (1977)

MS 2068: Original manuscript of *Gone*, 1977.
MS 2069: Untitled corrected typescript of *Gone*, not dated.
MS 2070: Untitled corrected typescript of *Gone* with stage directions, 1977.
MS 2071: Xerox copy of printed text of *Gone* under the title *A Piece of Monologue*.
MS 2072: Untitled original manuscript of *Gone*, 1977.
MS 2604: Typescript of *Solo*, Samuel Beckett's translation of *A Piece of Monologue* into French, not dated.

Catastrophe (1982)

MS 2456: Three corrected typescripts of *Catastrophe* in French, not dated.
MS 2457: Two manuscript drafts of *Catastrophe* in French, not dated.
MS 2458: Manuscript draft of *Catastrophe* in English, 1 May 1982.
MS 2464: Xerox copy of corrected typescript of *Catastrophe*, 1 July 1982.

Company (1979)

MS 1822: Original manuscript of the English and French texts of *Company/Compagnie*, 1977–9.

BIBLIOGRAPHY

Come and Go (1965)

MS 1227/7/16/4: Manuscript of part of a play in English entitled *Good Heavens*, not dated. Inscribed by Beckett 'Before *Come and Go*'.

MS 1227/7/16/5: Untitled corrected typescript of part of an early version of *Come and Go* involving three characters, Viola, Poppy and Rose, not dated.

MS 1533/1–4: Series of corrected typescripts of *Come and Go*.

MS 1532/1: Photocopy of the original manuscript of *Va et vient*, the author's translation of *Come and Go* into French, 21 March 1965.

MS 1532/2–3: Photocopies of corrected typescripts of *Va et vient*.

MS 1730: Production notebook for productions of *Kommen und Gehen* (Come and Go), *Eh Joe*, *Happy Days* and *Spiel* (Play) directed by Samuel Beckett, 1978.

Dream of Fair to Middling Women (1932)

MS 1227/7/16/9: Typescript copy of a photocopy of the corrected typescript of an unpublished novel, *Dream of Fair to Middling Women*, prepared by Nicholas Zurbrugg.

Eleutheria (1947)

MS 1227/7/4/1: Photocopy of a typescript of *Eleuthéria*, a three-act play in French by Samuel Beckett, copied from a typescript in the possession of A.J. Leventhal. c. 1947.

Footfalls (1975)

MS 1552/1: Original manuscript of *Footfalls* entitled *Footfalls It All?* 2 March, 1 and 25 October 1975.

MS 11552/2–6: Series of corrected typescripts of *Footfalls*.

MS 1976: Production Notebook containing notes by Samuel Beckett for productions of *Footfalls*, *That Time* and *Play*, at the Royal Court Theatre, London, and at the Schiller-Theater, Berlin, 1976.

Not I (1972)

MS 1227/7/12/1: Untitled original manuscript of *Not I*, 20 March 1972.

MS 1227/7/12/2–8: Series of corrected typescripts of *Not I*.

MS 1227/7/12/9: Photocopy of an uncorrected rehearsal script of *Not I*.

MS 1227/7/12/10: Typescript synopsis of *Not I*.

MS 1396/4/25: Untitled original manuscript of Samuel Beckett's translation of *Not I* into French 1–13 March 1973.

Ohio Impromptu (1981)

MS 2259: Xerox copy of the original manuscript, corrected typescript and final uncorrected typescript of *Ohio Impromptu*, c.1981.

MS 2260: Original manuscript and corrected typescript of Samuel Beckett's translation of *Ohio Impromptu* into French, c.1981.

Play (1962)

MS 1227/7/16/6: Untitled corrected typescript of a play in English involving three characters, Syke, Conk and Nickie, inscribed by Samuel Beckett 'Before *PLAY*', not dated.
MS 1528/1–11: Photocopy of a series of typescripts of *Play*.
MS 1227/7/13/1: Manuscript note by Samuel Beckett giving instructions for the repeat of *Play*, not dated.
MS 1581/15: Photocopy of manuscript notes by Georges Devine for the first production of *Play* in England, presented at the Old Vic, London, 1964.
MS 1531/2: Photocopy of the original manuscript of *Comédie*, Samuel Beckett's translation of *Play* into French, April–May 1963.
MS 1534/1–3: Photocopy of a series of corrected typescripts of *Comédie*.

What Where (1983)

MS 2603: Manuscript of *What Where*, Samuel Beckett's translation of *Quoi Où* into English, 12 May 1983.

Rockaby (1980)

MS 2196: Original manuscript of *Rockaby*, not dated.
MS 2197: Corrected typescript of *Rockaby*, not dated.
MS 2261: Original manuscript and corrected typescript of *Berceuse*, Samuel Beckett's translation of *Rockaby* into French, c.1982.

That Time (1974)

MS 1477/1: Original manuscript of *That Time*, 8–18 June 1974.
MS 1477/2–10: Series of corrected typescripts of *That Time*.
MS 1639: Original manuscript of stage directions of *That Time*.
MS 1657: Manuscript and two corrected typescripts of *Cette fois*, Samuel Beckett's translation of *That Time* into French, not dated.

PUBLISHED PROSE TEXTS BY SAMUEL BECKETT

This is not intended to be a complete list, but lists only the major prose works available in published form. References to Beckett's critical writings, apart from *Proust and Three Dialogues with Georges Duthuit*, are to the collection in *Disjecta: Miscellaneous writings and a Dramatic Fragment*, ed. Ruby Cohn. Quotations from the English text of shorter prose works or fragments are generally from *The Collected Shorter Prose 1945–80*, London, Calder, 1984.

Assez, Paris, Editions de Minuit, 1966.

Bing, Paris, Editions de Minuit, 1966.

Comment c'est, Paris, Editions de Minuit, 1961.

Company, London, Calder, 1980.

Le Dépeupleur, Paris, Editions de Minuit, 1970.

From an Abandoned Work, London, Faber and Faber, 1958.

Imagination morte imaginez, Paris, Editions de Minuit, 1965.

L'Innommable, Paris, Editions de Minuit, 1953.

Malone meurt, Paris, Editions de Minuit, 1951.

Mal vu mal dit, Paris, Editions de Minuit, 1981.

Mercier et Camier, Paris, Editions de Minuit, 1970.

Molloy, Paris, Editions de Minuit, 1951.

More Pricks Than Kicks (London, Chatto and Windus, 1934) London, Calder and Boyars, 1970.

Murphy, (London, Routledge, 1938) London, Calder, 1963.

Nouvelles et textes pour rien, Paris, Editions de Minuit, 1955.

Pour finir encore et autres foirades, Paris, Editions de Minuit, 1976.

Proust, (London, Dolphin Books, Chatto and Windus, 1931) in *Proust and Three Dialogues with Georges Duthuit*, London, Calder, 1965.

Sans, Paris, Editions de Minuit, 1969.

Three Dialogues with Georges Duthuit (*Transition*, December 1949) in *Proust and Three Dialogues with Georges Duthuit*, London, Calder, 1965.

Watt (Paris, Olympia Press, 1953) London, Calder, 1963.

Worstward Ho, London, Calder, 1983.

PUBLISHED TEXTS BY SAMUEL BECKETT FOR THE THEATRE, TELEVISION, RADIO, AND FILM

The English texts of later works and English versions of texts originally composed in French are usually quoted from *The Collected Shorter Plays of Samuel Beckett*, London, Faber and Faber, 1984, henceforth cited as *The Collected Shorter Plays*. Since I am listing editions of texts in both English and French, it seemed to make for greater comprehensibility in this section to refer only to readily available collections, particularly of the shorter works.

Actes sans paroles, in *Fin de Partie suivie de Actes sans paroles*, Paris, Editions de Minuit, 1957. (*Act without Words I and II*, in *Collected Shorter Plays*, London, Faber, 1986.)

All That Fall, London, Faber and Faber, 1957.

A Piece of Monologue, in *Collected Shorter Plays*.

Breath, in *Collected Shorter Plays*.

. . . but the clouds . . . in *Collected Shorter Plays*.

Cascando in *Collected Shorter Plays*.

Catastrophe in *Collected Shorter Plays*.

Come and Go, in *Collected Shorter Plays*.

Embers, in *Krapp's Last Tape* and *Embers*, London, Faber and Faber, 1959.

Eh Joe in *Collected Shorter Plays*.

En Attendant Godot, Paris, Editions de Minuit, 1952. (*Waiting for Godot*, London, Faber and Faber, 1956.)

Esquisse radiophonique, in *Pas suivi de quatre esquisses*, Paris, Editions de Minuit, 1978, henceforth cited as *Pas*. (*Rough for Radio I* in *Collected Shorter Plays*.)

Film in *Collected Shorter Plays*.

Fin de Partie, in *Fin de partie suivie de Actes sans paroles*, Paris, Editions de Minuit, 1957. (*Endgame*, London, Faber and Faber, 1958.)

Footfalls, in *Collected Shorter Plays*.

Fragments de Théatre I et II, in *Pas*. (*Rough for Theatre I and II*, in *Collected Shorter plays*.)

Ghost Trio, in *Collected Shorter Plays*.

Happy Days, London, Faber and Faber, 1962.

Krapp's Last Tape, in *Krapp's Last Tape* and *Embers*, London, Faber and Faber, 1959.

Nacht und Traüme, in *Collected Shorter Plays*.

Not I, in *Collected Shorter Plays*.

Ohio Impromptu, in *Collected Shorter Plays*.

Play, in *Collected Shorter Plays*.

Pochade Radiophonique, in *Pas*. (*Rough for Radio II*, in *Collected Shorter Plays*.)

Quad I and II, in *Collected Shorter Plays*.

Quoi Où, in *C.a.d.* (*What Where* in *Collected Shorter Plays*.)

Rockaby, in *Collected Shorter Plays*.

That Time, in *Collected Shorter Plays*.

Words and Music, in *Collected Shorter Plays*.

COLLECTED EDITIONS CONSULTED

Collected Shorter Plays of Samuel Beckett, London, Faber, 1986.

Collected Shorter Prose 1945–1980, London, Calder, 1984.

Collected Poems 1930–78, London, Calder, 1984.

Disjecta: Miscellaneous Writings and a Dramatic Fragment, ed. Ruby Cohn, London, Calder, 1983.

CRITICAL STUDIES OF SAMUEL BECKETT'S WORK

This listing is of necessity selected and includes only material of relevance to this study.

Acheson, James and Katerina Arthur, eds, *Beckett's Later Fiction and Drama: Texts for Company*, London, Macmillan, 1987.

Admussen, Richard, 'The manuscripts of Beckett's *Play*' *Modern Drama*, XVI, 1973, pp. 23–7.

Admussen, Richard, *The Samuel Beckett Manuscripts: A Study*, Boston, G.K. Hall, 1979.

Adorno, Theodor W., 'Trying to Understand *Endgame*', trans. Michael T. Jones, *New German Critique*, 26, Spring/Summer 1982, pp. 119–50.

Asmus, Walter, 'Rehearsal Notes for the German première of *That Time* and *Footfalls* at the Schiller-Theater Werkstatt, Berlin', *Journal of Beckett Studies*, 2, Summer 1977, pp. 82–95.

Astier, Pierre, 'Beckett's *Ohio Impromptu*: A View from the Isle of Swans', *Modern Drama*, XXV, 3, September 1982, pp. 331–48.

Avigal, S., 'Beckett's *Play*: The Circular Line of Existence', *Modern Drama*, XVIII, 1975, pp. 251–8.

Beja, Morris, S.E. Gontarski and Pierre Astier, eds, *Samuel Beckett: Humanistic Perspectives*, Columbus, Ohio State University Press, 1983.

Ben-Zvi, Linda, 'Samuel Beckett, Fritz Mauthner and the Limits of Language', *PMLA*, 95, March 1980, pp. 183–200.

Ben-Zvi, Linda, 'The Schismatic Self in *A Piece of Monologue*', *Journal of Beckett Studies*, 7, Spring 1982, pp. 7–18.

Ben-Zvi, Linda, *Samuel Beckett*, Boston, Twayne, 1986.

Ben-Zvi, Linda, ed., *Women in Beckett: Performance and Critical Perspectives*, Urbana, University of Illinois Press, 1990.

Blau, Herbert, 'The Bloody Show and the Eye of Prey: Beckett and Deconstruction', *Theatre Journal*, March 1987, pp. 5–19.

Brater, Enoch, 'The I in Beckett's *Not I*', *Twentieth Century Literature*, XX, 3, July 1974, pp. 189–200.

Brater, Enoch, 'Fragment and Form in *That Time* and *Footfalls*', *Journal of Beckett Studies*, 2, Summer 1977, pp. 70–81.

Brater, Enoch, 'A Footnote to Footfalls: Footsteps of Infinity on Beckett's Narrow Space', *Comparative Drama*, XXII, I, Spring 1978, pp. 35–41.

Brater, Enoch, 'Light, Sound, Movement and Action in Beckett's *Rockaby*', *Modern Drama*, XXV, September 1982, pp. 342–8.

Brater, Enoch, *Beyond Minimalism*, New York, Oxford University Press, 1986.

Brater, Enoch, ed., *Beckett at 80: Beckett in Context*, New York, Oxford University Press, 1986.

Burkman, Katherine, ed., *Myth and Ritual in the Plays of Samuel Beckett*, New Jersey, Associated University Presses, 1987.

Chabert, Pierre, 'Beckett as Director', *Gambit: International Theater Review*, 28, 1976, pp. 41–63.

Chabert, Pierre, 'The Body in Beckett's Theatre', *Journal of Beckett Studies*, 8, Autumn 1982, pp. 23–8.

Chabert, Pierre, ed., *Revue d'Esthétique*, numéro spéciale Beckett hors série, Toulouse, Editions Privat, 1986.

Cleveland, Louise O., 'Trials in the Soundscape: the Radio Plays of Samuel Beckett', *Modern Drama*, XI, 1968, pp. 267–82.

Coe, Richard, *Beckett*, Edinburgh, Oliver and Boyd, 1964, revised 1968.

Cohn, Ruby, 'Plays and Players in the Plays of Samuel Beckett', *Yale French Studies*, XXIX, Spring–Summer 1962, pp. 43–8.

Cohn, Ruby, *Back to Beckett*, Princeton, Princeton University Press, 1973.

Cohn, Ruby, 'Outward Bound Soliloquys', *Journal of Modern Literature*, VI, I, February 1977.

Cohn, Ruby, *Just Play: Beckett's Theatre*, Princeton, Princeton University Press, 1980.

Cohn, Ruby, ed., *Casebook on Waiting for Godot*, London, Macmillan, 1987.

Connor, Steven, *Samuel Beckett: Repetition, Theory and Text*, Oxford, Blackwell, 1988.

Dearlove, Judith, 'The Voice and its Words: How it is in Beckett's Canon', *Journal of Beckett Studies*, 3, Summer 1978, pp. 56–75.

Dearlove Judith, *Samuel Beckett's Nonrelational Art*, Durham, Duke University Press, 1982.

Elam, Keir , '*Not I*: Beckett's Mouth and the Ars(e) Rhetorica', in *Beckett at 80: Beckett in Context*, ed. E. Brater, New York, Oxford University Press, 1986.

Eliopolus, James, *Samuel Beckett's Dramatic Language*, The Hague, Mouton, 1975.

Esslin, Martin, ed., *A Collection of Critical Essays*, New Jersey, Prentice Hall, 1965.

Esslin, Martin, *Mediations*, Baton Rouge, Louisiana State University Press, 1980.

Esslin, Martin, 'Samuel Beckett and the Art of Broadcasting', *Encounter*, September 1985, pp. 38–44.

Federman, Raymond and Lawrence Graver, eds, *Samuel Beckett: the Critical Heritage*, London, Routledge & Kegan Paul, 1979.

Fehsenfeld, Martha, 'Everything Out but the Faces: Beckett's Reshaping of *What Where* for Television', *Modern Drama*, XXIX, 2, June 1986, pp. 229–40.

Fehsenfeld, Martha and Dougald MacMillan, *Beckett in the Theatre*, London, Calder, 1988.

Finney, Brian, *Since How It Is: A Study of Samuel Beckett's Later Fiction*, London, Covent Garden Press, 1972.

Fischer, E., 'The Discourse of the Other *Not I*: A Confluence of Beckett and Lacan', *Theatre*, 10, 3, Summer 1979, pp. 101–3.

Fletcher, Beryl, John Fletcher, Barry Smith and Walter Bachem, eds., *A Student's Guide to the Plays of Samuel Beckett*, London, Faber and Faber, 1978, revised 1985.

Fletcher, John and John Spurling, *Beckett: A Study of his Plays*, London, Eyre Methuen, 1972.

Free, William, 'Beckett's Plays and the Photographic Vision', *Georgia Review*, XXXIV, 4, Winter 1980, pp. 801–12.

Friedman, Alan, Charles Rossman and Dina Sherzer, eds., *Beckett Translating: Translating Beckett*, University Park, Pennsylvania State University Press, 1987.

Friedman, Melvin, ed., *Samuel Beckett Now*, Chicago, Il, University of Chicago Press, 1970.

Garner, Stanton B., 'Visual Field in Beckett's Late Plays', *Comparative Drama*, XXI, 4, Winter 1987–8, pp. 349–73.

Gidal, Peter, *Understanding Beckett*, London, Macmillan, 1986.

Gontarski, S.E. 'Making Yourself All Up Again: The Composition of Samuel Beckett's *That Time*', *Modern Drama*, XXIII, 1, Spring 1983, pp. 112–20.

Gontarski, S.E., *The Intent of Undoing in Samuel Beckett's Dramatic Texts*, Bloomington, Indiana University Press, 1985.

Gontarski, S.E., ed, *On Beckett: Essays and Criticism*, New York, Grove Press, 1986.

Hale, Jane A., *The Broken Window: Beckett's Dramatic Perspective*, Indiana, Purdue University Press, 1987.

Harvey, Laurence, *Samuel Beckett: Poet and Critic*, Princeton, Princeton University Press, 1970.

Hayman, Ronald, *Samuel Beckett*, London, Heineman, 1968.

Hoffman, Frederick J., *Samuel Beckett: The Language of Self*, Carbondale, Il, Southern Illinois University Press, 1962.

Homan, Sidney, *Beckett's Theaters: Interpretations for Performance*, Lewisburg, Bucknell University Press and Associated University Presses, 1984.

Hubert, Renée Riese, 'Beckett's *Play*: Between Poetry and Performance', *Modern Drama*, IX, December 1966, pp. 339–46.

Iser, Wolfgang, 'Samuel Beckett's Dramatic Language', trans. Ruby Cohn, *Modern Drama*, IX, December 1966, pp. 251–9.

Kalb, Jonathan, *Beckett in Performance*, Cambridge, Cambridge University Press, 1989.

Kelly, Katherine, 'The Orphic Mouth in *Not I*' *Journal of Beckett Studies*, 5, Autumn 1979, pp. 45–68.

Kenner, Hugh, *A Reader's Guide to Samuel Beckett*, New York, Farrar, Straus and Giraux, 1973.

Knowlson, James, *Light and Darkness in the Theatre of Samuel Beckett*, London, Turret Books, 1972.

Knowlson, James and John Pilling, *Frescoes of the Skull*, London, Calder, 1979.

Knowlson, James, ed., *Theater Workbook I: Krapp's Last Tape*, London, Brutus Books, 1980.

Knowlson, James, 'Beckett's "Bits of Pipe" ', in *Samuel Beckett: Humanistic Perspectives*, ed. M. Beja, S. E. Gontarski and P. Astier, Columbus, Ohio State University Press, 1983.

Knowlson, James, 'Ghost Trio/Geister Trio' in *Beckett at 80: Beckett in Context*, ed. E. Brater, New York, Oxford University Press, 1986.

Laughlin, Karen, 'Beckett's Three Dimensions: Narration, Dialogue and the Role of the Reader in *Play*', *Modern Drama*, XXVIII, 3, pp. 329–40.

Lawley, Paul, 'Symbolic Structure and Creative Obligation in *Endgame*', *Journal of Beckett Studies*, 5, Autumn 1979, pp. 45–68.

Lawley, Paul, 'Beckett's Dramatic Counterpoint: a reading of *Play*', *Journal of Beckett Studies*, 9, pp. 25–41.

Lawley, Paul, 'Counterpoint, Absence and the Medium in Beckett's *Not I*', *Modern Drama*, XXVI, December 1983, pp. 407–13.

Lawley, Paul, unpublished article, 'Footfalls and Audience'.

Libera, Antoni, 'Structure and Pattern in *That Time*', *Journal of Beckett Studies*, 6, Autumn 1980, pp. 81–9.

Libera, Antoni, 'Beckett's *Catastrophe*', *Modern Drama*, September 1985, pp. 341–7.

Lyons, Charles, 'Perceiving *Rockaby* – As a Text, As a Text by Samuel Beckett, As a Text for Performance', *Comparative Drama*, 16, 4, Winter 1982–3, pp. 297–311.

Lyons, Charles, *Samuel Beckett*, New York, Grove Press, 1983.

Morrison, Kristin, 'The Rip Word in *A Piece of Monologue*', *Modern Drama*, XXV, September 1982, pp. 349–54.

Morrison, Kristin, *Canters and Chronicles: The Use of Narrative in the Plays of Samuel Beckett and Harold Pinter*, Chicago, University of Chicago Press, 1983.

O'Donovan, Patrick, 'Beckett's monologues: The Context and Conditions of Representation', *Modern Language Review*, 81, 1986, pp. 318–26.

Pilling, John, *Samuel Beckett*, London, Routledge & Kegan Paul, 1976.

Pilling, John, 'The Significance of Beckett's *Still*', *Essays in Criticism*, XXVIII, 2, April 1978, pp. 143–57.

Porter Abbott, H. 'Tyranny and Theatricality', *Theatre Journal*, March 1988.

Postlewait, Thomas, 'Self-Performing Voices: Mind, Memory and Time in Beckett's Drama', *Twentieth Century Literature*, XXIV, Winter 1978, pp. 473–91.

Pountney, Rosemary, 'Samuel Beckett's Interest in Form: Structural Pattering in *Play*', *Modern Drama*, XIX, 1976, pp. 237–44.

Pountney, Rosemary, *Theatre of Shadows: Samuel Beckett's Drama 1956–76*, Irish Literary Studies, Colin Smythe, 1988.

Rabinovitz, Rubin, 'Time, Space and Verisimilitude in Samuel Beckett's Fiction', *Journal of Beckett Studies*, 2, Summer 1977, pp. 40–6.

Rabinovitz, Rubin, *The Development of Samuel Beckett's Fiction*, Champaign, University of Illinois Press, 1984.

Revue d'Esthètique, Samuel Beckett, ed. Pierre Chabert, numéro spécial hors série, avril 1986.

Rotjman, Betty, *Forme et signification dans le théatre de Beckett*, Paris, Nizet, 1976.

Simone, R. Thomas, ' "Faint, though by no means invisible": A Commentary on *Footfalls*', *Modern Drama*, XXVI, December 1983, pp. 435–46.

Soloman, Philip H. 'Purgatory Unpurged: Time, Space and Language in *Lessness*', *Journal of Beckett Studies*, 6, Autumn 1980, pp. 63–72.

States, Bert O., *The Shape of Paradox: An Essay on Waiting for Godot*, Berkeley, University of California Press, 1978.

States, Bert O., '*Catastrophe*: Beckett's Laboratory/Theater', *Modern Drama*, XXX, I, March 1987.

Takahashi, Yasunari, 'Samuel Beckett and the Noh', *Encounter*, LVIII, 4, April 1982, pp. 66–73.

Watson, David, *Paradox and Desire in Beckett's Fiction*, London, Macmillan, 1991.

Watt, Stephen, 'Beckett by Way of Baudrillard: Toward a Political Reading of Samuel Beckett's Drama', in *Myth and Ritual in the Plays of Samuel Beckett*, ed. Katherine Burkman, New Jersey, Associated University Presses, 1987.

Webb, Eugene, *The Plays of Samuel Beckett*, Seattle, University of Washington Press, 1972.

Worth, Katherine, ed., *Beckett the Shape Changer*, London, Routledge & Kegan Paul, 1975.

Worthen, William B., 'Playing *Play*', *Modern Drama*, XXVI, 4, December 1983, pp. 415–24.

Zeifman, Hersch, '*Come and Go*: "A Criticule" ', in *Samuel Beckett: Human-*

istic Perspectives, ed. M. Beja, S. E. Gontarski and P. Astier, Columbus, OH, Ohio State University Press, 1983.

Zeifman, Hersch, 'Being and Non-Being in Samuel Beckett's *Not I*', *Modern Drama*, XIX, 1976, pp. 35–46.

Zeifman, Hersch, ' "The Core of the Eddy": *Rockaby* and Dramatic Genre', in *Beckett Translating: Translating Beckett*, eds, A. Friedman, C. Rossman and D. Sherzer, University Park, PA, Pennsylvania State University Press, 1987.

Zilliacus, Clas, 'Samuel Beckett's *Embers*: A Matter of Fundamental Sounds', *Modern Drama*, XIII, 1970, pp. 216–25.

Zilliacus, Clas, *Beckett and Broadcasting: A Study of the Works of Samuel Beckett for and in Radio and Television*, Abo, Finland, Abo Akademi, 1976.

OTHER WORKS CONSULTED

Adorno, Theodor, *Aesthetic Theory*, trans. C. Lenhardt, London, Routledge & Kegan Paul, 1984.

Anderson, Linda, 'At the Threshold of the Self: Women and Autobiography', in *Women's Writing: A Challenge to Theory*, ed. Moira Monteith, Brighton, Harvester Press, 1986.

Artaud, Antonin, *Le Théâtre et son double*, Paris, Editions Gallimard, Oeuvres Complètes, Tome IV.

Auslander, Philip, 'Towards a Concept of the Political in Postmodern Theatre', *Theatre Journal*, March 1987.

Bachelard, Gaston, *La Poétique de l'espace*, Paris, Presses Universitaires de France, 1957.

Bakhtin, Mikhail, *The Dialogic Imagination*, ed. Michael Holquist, trans. Caryl Emerson and Michael Holquist, Austin, The University of Texas Press, 1981.

Bann, Stephen and John E. Bowlt, eds, *Russian Formalism*, Edinburgh, Scottish Academic Press, 1973.

Barthes, Roland, 'Barthes in Theatre', *Theatre Quarterly*, IX, 33, pp. 25–30.

Barthes, Roland, *On Racine*, trans. Richard Howard, New York, Performing Arts Journal Publications, 1983.

Barthes, Roland, *Image-Music-Text*, trans. Stephen Heath, London, Fontana, 1977.

Bassnet-McGuire, Susan, 'An Introduction to Theatre Semiotics', *Theatre Quarterly*, X, 38, Summer 1980, pp. 47–53.

Belsey, Catherine, *Critical Practice*, London, Methuen, 1985.

Benvenuto, Bice and Roger Kennedy, *The Works of Jacques Lacan: An Introduction*, London, Free Association Books, 1986.

Blau, Herbert, *Take Up The Bodies: Theatre at the Vanishing Point*, Urbana, IL, University of Illinois Press, 1982.

Bloom, Harold et al., eds, *Deconstruction and Criticism*, London, Routledge & Kegan Paul, 1979.

Bogatyrev, Petr, 'Les signes du théâtre', *Poétique*, 8, 1971, pp. 517–30.

Bradby, David, *Modern French Drama, 1940–80*, Cambridge, Cambridge University Press, 1984.

Braidotti, Rosi, *Patterns of Dissonance*, Cambridge, Polity Press, 1991.

BIBLIOGRAPHY

Brennan, Teresa, ed., *Between Feminism and Psychoanalysis*, London, Routledge, 1989.

Brewer, Maria Minich, 'Performing Theory', *Theatre Journal*, 37, 1985, pp. 13–30.

Brook, Peter, *The Empty Space*, Harmondsworth, Penguin, 1972.

Butler, Judith, *Gender Trouble*, London, Routledge, 1990.

Case, Sue-Ellen, ed., *Performing Feminisms: Feminist Critical Theory and Theatre*, Baltimore, Johns Hopkins University Press, 1990.

Casey, Edward, 'Imagination and Repetition in Literature: A Reassessment', *Yale French Studies*, 52, 1975, pp. 249–67.

Chaikin, Joseph, *The Presence of the Actor*, New York, Atheneum, 1972.

Chatman, Seymour, *Story and Discourse: Narrative Structure in Fiction and Film*, Ithaca, NY, Cornell University Press, 1978.

Ciulei, Liviu, 'L'Eclairage et le son dans l'espace théâtrale, *Travail Théâtral*, 14, January–March, 1974, pp. 30–3.

Cixous, Hélène and Catherine Clément, *The Newly Born Woman* trans. Betsy Wing, Manchester, Manchester University Press, 1986.

Coleridge, Samuel Taylor, *Biographia Literaria*, London, J.M. Dent, 1906.

Cook, Carol, 'Unbodied Figures of Desire', *Theatre Journal*, March 1986, pp. 34–52.

Corvin, Michel, 'Contribution à l'analyse de l'espace scénique dans le théâtre contemporain', *Travail Théâtral*, 22, January–March 1976, pp. 62–80.

Culler, Jonathan, *Structuralist Poetics*, London, Routledge & Kegan Paul, 1975.

Davies, Robert Con, 'Introduction', *Modern Language Notes*, December 1983, 'Lacan and Narration: The Psychoanalytic Difference in Narrative Theory'.

Deleuze, Gilles, *Différence et répétition*, Paris, Presses Universitaires de France, 1968.

Deleuze, Gilles and Féliz Guattari, *Capitalisme et Schizophrénie, I: L'Anti-Oedipe*, Paris, Editions de Minuit, 1972.

Derrida, Jacques, *Writing and Difference*, trans. Alan Bass, London, Routledge, 1978.

Derrida, Jacques, *Dissemination*, trans. Barbara Johnson, London, Athlone Press, 1981.

Derrida, Jacques, 'LIVING ON: *Borderlines*', in *Deconstruction and Criticism*, ed. Harold Bloom, London, Routledge & Kegan Paul, 1979.

Diamond, Elin, 'Mimesis, Mimicry and the True-real', in *Modern Drama*, XXXII, 1, 1989, pp. 58–72.

Dreyfus, Hubert L. and Paul Rabinow, *Michel Foucault: Beyond Structuralism and Hermeneutics*, Brighton, Harvester Press, 1982.

Eagleton, Terry, *Literary Theory: An Introduction*, Oxford, Blackwell, 1983.

Elam, Keir, *The Semiotics of Theatre and Drama*, London, Methuen, 1980.

Féral, Josette, 'Performance and Theatricality', trans. Teresa Lyons, *Modern Drama*, XXV, 1, 1982, pp. 170–81.

Finter, Helga, 'Experimental Theatre and Semiology of Theatre: The Theatricalisation of Voice', *Modern Drama*, XXVI, 4, December. 1983, pp. 501–17.

Foster, Hal, ed., *The Anti-Aesthetic: Essays on Postmodern Culture*, Port Townsend, Bay Press, 1985.

Foster, Susan, 'The Signifying Body: Reaction and Resistance in Postmodern Dance', *Theatre Journal*, March 1985, pp. 45–64.

Foucault, Michel, *Discipline and Punish: The Birth of the Prison*, trans. Alan Sheridan, Harmondsworth, Penguin, 1977.

Foucault, Michel, 'Nietzsche, Genealogy, History', in *The Foucault Reader*, ed. Paul Rabinow, Harmondsworth, Penguin, 1986.

Foucault, Michel, 'Of Other Spaces', *Diacritics*, Spring 1986, pp. 22–7.

Freedman, Barbara, 'Frame-Up: Feminism, Psychoanalysis, Theatre', in *Performing Feminisms: Feminist Critical Theory and Theatre*, ed. Sue-Ellen Case, Baltimore, MD, Johns Hopkins University Press, 1990.

Freedman, Barbara, *Staging the Gaze: Postmodernism, Psychoanalysis and Shakespearean Comedy*, Ithaca, NY, Cornell University Press, 1991.

Freud, Sigmund, 'A Child is being Beaten', *The Penguin Freud Library*, 10, Harmondsworth, Penguin, 1979.

Freud, Sigmund, 'Beyond the Pleasure Principle', *The Penguin Freud Library*, 11, Harmondsworth, Penguin, 1984.

Freud, Sigmund, 'Melancholia and Mourning', *The Penguin Freud Library*, 11, Harmondsworth, Penguin, 1984.

Freud, Sigmund, 'The Ego and the Id', *The Penguin Freud Library*, 11, Harmondsworth, Penguin, 1984.

Fuchs, Eleanor, 'Presence and the Revenge of Writing: Rethinking Theatre After Derrida', *Performing Arts Journal*, 26/27, 1985, pp. 163–73.

Gallop, Jane, *Reading Lacan*, Ithaca, NY, Cornell University Press, 1985.

Garner, Stanton B., 'Visual Field in Beckett's Late Plays', *Comparative Drama*, XXI, 4, Winter 1987–8.

Genette, Gérard, *Figures of Literary Discourse*, trans. Alan Sheridan, Oxford, Blackwell, 1982.

Harvey, David, *The Condition of Postmodernity*, Oxford, Blackwell, 1989.

Hawkes, Terence, *Structuralism and Semiotics*, London, Methuen, 1977.

Helbo, Andre, 'Theater as Representation', *Sub-stance*, 18/19, 1977, pp. 172–81.

Holub, Robert C., *Reception Theory: A Critical Introduction*, London, Methuen, 1984.

Ingarden, Roman, 'Les fonctions du langage au théatre', *Poétique*, 8, 1971, pp. 531–8.

Irigaray, Luce, *This Sex Which Is Not One*, trans. Catherine Porter, Ithaca, NY, Cornell University Press, 1985.

Irigaray, Luce, *The Irigaray Reader*, ed. Margaret Whitford, Oxford, Blackwell, 1991.

Issacharoff, Michael, 'Space and Reference in Drama', *Poetics Today*, 2, 3, 1981.

Jacobus, Mary, *Reading Woman*, London, Methuen, 1986.

Jakobson, Roman, *Essai de linguistique générale*, Paris, Editions de Minuit, 1970.

Jamieson, Frederick, 'Imaginary and Symbolic in Lacan: Marxism, Psychoanalytic Criticism and the Problem of the Subject', *Yale French Studies*, 55–6, 1977, pp. 338–95.

Jardine, Alice, *Gynesis: Configurations of Woman and Modernity*, Ithaca, NY, Cornell University Press, 1985.

Klein, Melanie, *The Selected Melanie Klein*, ed. Juliet Mitchell, Harmondsworth, Penguin, 1986.

Kristeva, Julia, *Revolution in Poetic Language*, trans. Margaret Waller, New York, Columbia University Press, 1984.

Kristeva, Julia, 'The Ruin of a Poetics', in *Russian Formalism*, ed. Stephen Bann and John E. Bowlt, Edinburgh, Scottish Academic Press, 1973.

Kristeva, Julia, 'Modern Theater Does Not Take (A) Place', *Sub-stance* 18/19, 1977, pp. 131–4.

Kristeva, Julia, *Desire in Language: A Semiotic Approach to Literature and Art*, Oxford, Blackwell, 1980.

Krupnick, Mark, ed., *Displacement: Derrida and After*, Bloomington, Indiana University Press, 1983.

Krysinski, Wladimir, 'Semiotic Modalities of the Body in Modern Drama', *Poetics Today*, II, 3, Spring 1981, pp. 141–61.

Lacan, Jacques, 'Some Reflections on the Ego', *International Journal of Psychoanalysis*, 34, 1953.

Lacan, Jacques, *Ecrits: A Selection*, trans. Alan Sheridan, London, Tavistock, 1977.

Lacan, Jacques, *The Four Fundamental Concepts of Psychoanalysis*, trans. Alan Sheridan, Harmondsworth, Penguin, 1977.

Lebovici, Serge and Daniel Widlocher, *Psychoanalysis in France*, New York, International University Press, 1980.

Lemaire, Anika, *Jacques Lacan*, trans. David Macey, London, Routledge & Kegan Paul, 1977.

Lentriccia, Frank, *After the New Criticism*, London Athlone Press, 1980.

MacCannell, Juliet Flower, *The Regime of the Brother*, London, Routledge, 1991.

Mallarmé, Stéphane, *Divagations*, Paris, Bibliotheque Charpentier, 1949.

Matoré, Georges, *L'Espace Humaine*, La Colombe, Collection Sciences et Techniques Humaines, 1962.

Megill, Allan, *Prophets of Extremity: Nietzsche, Heidegger, Foucault, Derrida*, Berkeley, CA, University of California Press, 1985.

Melançon, Joseph, 'Theatre as Semiotic Practice', *Modern Drama*, XXV, 1, March 1982, pp. 17–24.

Mitchell, Juliet, *Psychoanalysis and Feminism*, Harmondsworth, Penguin, 1974.

Modern Language Notes, 'Lacan and Narration: The Psychoanalytic Difference in Narrative Theory', 98, 5, December 1983.

Monk, Philip, 'Common Carrier: Performance by Artists', *Modern Drama*, XXV, 1, 1982.

Montieth, Moira, ed., *Women's Writing: A Challenge to Theory*, Brighton, Harvester Press, 1986.

Muller, John P. and William J. Richardson, *Lacan and Language: A Reader's Guide to the Ecrits*, New York, International Universities Press, 1982.

Newham, Paul, 'The Voice and the Shadow', *Performance*, 60, Spring 1990.

Nietzsche, Friedrich, *Beyond Good and Evil*, Chicago, Gateway Editions, 1955.

Nietzsche, Friedrich, *The Birth of Tragedy and the Geneology of Morals*, New York, Anchor Books, 1956.

Nietzsche, Friedrich, *Thus Spake Zarathustra*, trans. R.J. Hollingdale, Harmondsworth Penguin, 1964.

Nietzsche, Friedrich, *The Will to Power*, ed. Walter Kaufmann, New York, Vintage Books, 1968.

Norris, Christopher, *Deconstruction: Theory and Practice*, London, Methuen, 1982.

Pavis, Patrice, 'The Classical Heritage of Modern Drama: The Case of Postmodern Theatre, *Modern Drama*, XXIX, 1, March 1986, pp. 1–22.

Pavis, Patrice, *Problemes de Sémiologie théatrale*, Paris, Les Presses Universitaires de France, 1978.

Poetics Today, 'Drama, Theatre, Performance', 2, 3, 1981.

Pontbriand, Chantal, 'The Eye Finds no Fixed Point at Which to Rest', *Modern Drama*, XXV, 1, 1982, pp. 154–62.

Poulet, Georges, *Etudes sur le temps humaines*, Edinburgh, Edinburgh University Press, 1949.

Proust, Marcel, *A la Recherche du temps perdu*, Paris, Gallimard, Editions de la Pléiade, 1954.

Schleifer, Ronald, 'The Space and Dialogue of Desire: Lacan, Greimas and Narrative Temporality', *Modern Language Notes*, 98, 5, December 1983.

Scholes, Robert, *Structuralism in Literature: An Introduction*, Yale University Press, 1974.

Sub-stance, 18/19, 1977, Theater in France, Ten years of Research.

Sturrock, John, ed., *Structuralism and Since: From Levi Strauss to Derrida*, Oxford, Oxford University Press, 1979.

Ubersfeld, Anne, *Lire le théâtre*, Paris, Editions Sociales, 1977.

Vernois, Paul, ed., *L'Onirisme et l'insolite dans le théâtre contemporain*, Paris, Editions Klinksieck, 1974.

Wright, Elizabeth, *Psychoanalytic Criticism: Theory in Practice*, London, Methuen, 1984.

Young, Robert, *Untying the Text: A Post-Structuralist Reader*, London, Routledge & Kegan Paul, 1981.

INDEX

151